GOD & MIND

Extraordinary Coexistence

GARY E. BELL

WESTBOW
PRESS®
A DIVISION OF THOMAS NELSON
& ZONDERVAN

WestBow Press books may be ordered through booksellers or by contacting:

WestBow Press
A Division of Thomas Nelson & Zondervan
1663 Liberty Drive
Bloomington, IN 47403
www.westbowpress.com
844-714-3454

ISBN: 978-1-6642-3061-3 (sc)
ISBN: 978-1-6642-3060-6 (e)

Print information available on the last page.

WestBow Press rev. date: 5/6/2021

CONTENTS

Acknowledgments vii

Introduction ix

Chapter 1   The Problem.. 1

Chapter 2   The Spirit of God Within Us...................................... 6

Chapter 3   Faith and The Power of Believing.............................11

Chapter 4   The Supercomputer..19

Chapter 5   Bad Code..32

Chapter 6   Foundations 42

Chapter 7   The Active Toolbox..50

Chapter 8   The Passive Toolbox...71

Summary...79

ACKNOWLEDGMENTS

To my family - my daughter Cassie, who edited the manuscript superbly, and gave me great comments and ideas; my son Marty, who conceptualized and produced the graphics for the cover; my son Ryan, who always offers encouragement and support; and to my wife Frannie, who supported me with her biblical knowledge and love. She is the love of my life.

INTRODUCTION

"Deep within man dwell those slumbering powers; powers that would astonish him, that he never dreamed of possessing; forces that would revolutionize his life if aroused and put into action." Orison Swett Marden, an American writer in the early twentieth century.

The Bible tells us that we were made in the image of God. That is quite an amazing statement in itself, but additionally, our brains are the most powerful supercomputers on the face of the earth, and we can use them to connect with God. So why is it that mankind, in general, views humanity as extremely limited in our capabilities and we continue to lead ordinary lives? The statement, *"After all, you're only human,"* encapsulates that pervasive thinking. The significant limitations of what we believe we are capable of are a result of thousands of years of accumulated belief, and it is exacerbated by the constant negative programming our brains receive every day. In reality, humans can do far more than we believe; however, to be successful in all aspects of life, we must connect with God and move past the generational beliefs and the negative programming that continue to hold us captive. These false beliefs result in fear and doubt deep within our minds.

Think about how amazing you could be if your internal fear and doubt were significantly reduced. Have you have ever met someone who is extremely confident in everything they do? You can almost see the confidence glowing in their face. They have somehow managed to bypass or ignore the negative programming. The amazing thing is, you can do it too, by using what I call the four cornerstones, to reprogram your mind to increase positive thoughts, decrease the negative ones, and reduce fear and doubt, leading to a successful and joyous life.

The first of the four cornerstones is to stay in constant contact with God, the almighty creator of the universe, which will awaken the spirit of God that is within you. The second is a basic philosophy of successful living that I call *Believing Like Christ* - having the pure faith of Christ. Jesus believed completely that God would provide whatever He asked from the Father and we should believe as He did. Believing as Jesus Christ did helps us to access the spirit of God that is within us and have complete and unwavering faith in what we can accomplish in our lives through the power of God. The third is the foundations that you build your life upon and how they affect you, and the fourth cornerstone is the toolbox that contains a variety of both active and passive tools specifically designed to reprogram your mind to reduce fear and doubt and add positive programming.

It is time to turn the page in the book of your life – to cease being held in bondage by fear and doubt, and to begin to be EXTRAORDINARY!

THE PROBLEM

"Too often we allow negative programming to control our lives. The good news is that through unrelenting determination, anything that is programmed can be reprogrammed to lead us to success."
Allen Weinstein, Entrepreneur and Author

For God did not give us a spirit of fear but a spirit of power, of love and of self-discipline. 2 Timothy 1:7

Human beings have untapped capabilities far above what we would consider normal when we are in constant communication with God. You are empowered through God in His image and have the built-in capacity to do amazing things, much greater than you could ever imagine. Mentally, emotionally, and spiritually, human beings have incredible capabilities that were given to us by the Creator that are far beyond what we currently consider normal.

The Bible tells us that we have the spirit of God in us (*But whoever is united with the Lord is one with him in spirit.* 1 Cor 6:17), but you must awaken it through prayer and meditation. When you are walking with God and believing, you are capable of extraordinary things. Philippians 4:13 states, *I can do all things through Christ who strengthens me,* and Ephesians 1:19-20 tells us of the *incomparably great power for us who believe. That power is the same as the mighty strength he exerted when he raised Christ from the dead.* This verse is saying that Christians have the power that raised Christ from the dead within us. That's a pretty compelling statement, but many Christians are unaware of it and other statements in the Bible about the power that is within you when you accept Christ and are walking with God. If you are not a Christian, I highly recommend reading the New Testament and seeing for yourself the amazing scriptures that show the power of God that is within you if you have accepted Christ as your Savior, and how to release it. I believe it will be as enlightening to you as it was to me, because for over 35 years I was not a Christian, and for probably 10 years after that I was a classic casual Christian. I relied on myself instead of using the power of God and relying on Him.

There are instances of people elevating their thoughts to levels rarely achieved by accessing the spirit of God within them through their subconscious minds. In these cases, human beings have had moments where they exhibited capabilities well beyond that expected of and normally exhibited by the human race, even if for just a very brief moment. A scientist working on a project has an epiphany that is a gigantic leap of thought and reasoning that leads to a significant breakthrough, an athlete gets "in the zone" and performs incredibly, a group or an individual prays and a miracle happens, a healing occurs, someone shows complete selflessness for a person or a cause, or a person somehow knows something through intuition. These are the times that, perhaps for a brief moment, we elevate ourselves from what is considered normal human being capabilities. We transcend the boundaries we have put on ourselves as human beings and extend significantly what we are capable of as a species.

Sadly, in many cases these capabilities emerge only sporadically and are largely untapped; we continue to live, in most cases, ordinary and difficult lives. The limitations we put on ourselves are based on what is passed on to us from generation to generation, and we conform to those expectations. But we were built for so much more; we were built in the image of God. So why do we not use our brains to their fullest extent? What has led us to this point? It is programming – the constant negative programming that saturates your brain.

Your mind is made up of two parts, the conscious mind and the subconscious mind. Your conscious mind is where you do your everyday thinking and short-term memory. The subconscious mind is where the power comes from; it is a supercomputer of almost unimaginable capability and accounts for most of your brain's computing power. But like any computer, it needs programming instructions, and it gets them from the conscious mind, interacting continuously with your conscious thoughts, taking visual and aural information from your conscious mind in every facet of your life, and it has been doing it every day since you were a small child. In lieu of inputs from your conscious mind, it retrieves memories embedded deeply in your subconscious. Your subconscious mind uses these programming instructions to make you become who you believe yourself to be. It will ensure that your success in all facets of your life directly correlates to your thoughts concerning how capable you believe you are, how high on the ladder of success you should ascend to, and what kind of person you should be.

One of the major problems with this process is that your conscious mind is bombarded daily with negative thoughts, negative comments from people (including family and friends), negative outcomes (mistakes, failures and embarrassing moments), and negative news and other information from various media and internet sources. From early on in life we are told of our limitations, and our belief in them and subsequent failures lead us to confirm these limitations.

Additionally, the media, in its various forms, gives us massive doses of negative programming. On social media sites we tend to see people at their worst, tearing each other apart in every possible way. When we watch television we see several ads every hour telling us what drugs we need to survive, what sickness and diseases we will probably get, and how difficult life is unless you have this product or that product. Watching or reading the news is no better – online estimates indicate that 90 percent of the stories are of a negative nature, because that is what sells. A recent survey from the American Psychological Association found that over half of all Americans say that watching the news causes them stress, anxiety, and fatigue or sleep loss, and it all seeps deep into our subconscious minds. And most movies and television shows are no better, showing humans killing, lying, cheating, stealing, scheming against others, and living a generally sinful life.

To be successful in life we must learn to diminish and disregard the negative programming, or "bad code" as I call it, and on a daily basis reprogram our minds in positive ways. Using the four cornerstones, the power of God that is inherent in all of us, pure faith, firm foundations, and some basic tools we can diminish and disregard negative programming and get closer to a pristine state of mind regarding the thoughts that determine our lives. Only then we will begin to experience life as God had intended, with strength, confidence, goodness and kindness. The tools are very simple and easy to use, but it will take a small amount of effort. Some results you will see immediately, some in a month or two, and some are long term. In any case, they are well worth the time spent. After all, if you can live an extraordinary life, why settle for ordinary?

Walking with God and accessing the spirit of God that lies within you plays a major part in achieving success and will produce a deep-seated joy in you that is missing in many people, even many casual Christians. It is a joy that sustains even in hard times. Before I became a Christian I had fun and enjoyed myself, but there was always something missing - a deep sustaining joy.

Having the faith of Christ allows us to use more of that 90% of unused brain capacity that you've always heard about (we'll dispel that myth later) and allow our subconscious mind to take over. Through a belief in God and the magnificent world he has created for us, we can do this, not just momentarily, but on a daily basis. When we believe like Jesus Christ we reduce fear and doubt and move closer towards fulfilling Christ's belief that we can elevate ourselves through God to a higher level of conscious thought, compassion, morality, and spirituality, and become closer to Christ and God the Creator. I believe this is God's will for mankind.

Putting the four cornerstones presented in this book into practice will increase your performance in all the areas of your life that you desire. Your spiritual and personal relationships will strengthen considerably and become much better. Your physical and mental health will get better. Your performance in personal endeavors, such as athletics, will increase. And you will see substantial positive changes in your professional life.

In whatever field you choose to pursue in life your performance need only be a small percentage better than the competition to be wildly more successful. In most cases, in any field, the performance differences between the best and the rest are very slight, but the rewards for success at the top are far greater. For instance, the world's greatest sprinter wins his races on the average of .1 seconds better than the others, yet he or she is a well-known superstar, while those that finish second or third are relatively unknown. A writer whose book is just a little better than others sells millions of copies instead of thousands. A CEO who makes hundreds of thousands or millions of dollars a year in salary and bonuses, in many cases was just a little better than his competition, who make much less than what he makes.

To get that edge, to get us just past the competition, we need to apply the four cornerstones and use the faith that is within us, because true faith is the most powerful force on the planet. If we can get past the historical beliefs of mankind's abilities, the negative programming, and the complexity of today's world, we will begin to see a significant difference.

2

THE SPIRIT OF GOD
WITHIN US

You, however, are not in the realm of the flesh but are in the
realm of the Spirit, if indeed the Spirit of God lives in you.
Romans 8:9

"Those who walk with God always reach their destination."
Henry Ford

First and foremost, in our search for the truth about our world and how to be successful in it, we must look to God, the creator of the universe. Staying in touch with the Creator on a daily basis and awakening the spirit of God that is within you, the Holy Spirit, is the first of our four cornerstones. I know that references to the Holy Spirit in secular circles and even in some Christian circles is seen as radical and "on the fringe", but God is spirit that is everywhere and the Holy Spirt is simply the spirit of God that dwells within each of us that remains dormant until you reach out to God and ask for it. Seeking the Holy Spirit is a prevailing theme throughout the New Testament and specifically by Jesus' words. Many references are made to the power of the Holy Spirit to transform us and help us to be closer to God and to think and conduct our lives like Christ.

...and to put on the new self, created to be like God in true righteousness and holiness.
(Eph 4:24)

And we all, who with unveiled faces contemplate the Lord's glory, are being transformed into his image with ever-increasing glory, which comes from the Lord, who is the Spirit. (2 Cor 3:18)

Ephesians 4:24 states that your newly created spirit is righteous and holy - it is perfect, just as Jesus was. That is a great motivator to be walking in the spirit instead of the flesh! The Holy Spirit is the connection to God through your spirit, which is accessed through your subconscious mind. It gives you intuitive knowledge, wisdom, patience, and virtue, and guides you in your walk of faith.

Jesus describes the Holy Spirit in the book of John:

"The Holy Spirit, whom the Father will send in my name, will teach you all things and will remind you of everything I have said to you." (John 14:26)

"And I will ask the Father, and he will give you another Advocate, who will never leave you. He is the Holy Spirit, who leads into all truth. The world cannot receive him, because it isn't looking for him and doesn't recognize him. But you know him, because he lives with you now and later will be in you." (John 14:16-17)

Jesus talks about the Holy Spirit being the spirit of truth, and that it was indwelling with the apostles once they believed as He did. Prior to receiving the Holy Spirit, the apostles were confused and afraid - remember when Peter denied Jesus three times. But it transformed them and enabled them to perform miracles the same as Jesus did. In fact, Jesus told them not to leave Jerusalem to preach until they received the Holy Spirit because He knew they would be transformed with power.

On one occasion, while he was eating with them, he gave them this command: "Do not leave Jerusalem, but wait for the gift my Father promised, which you have heard me speak about. (Acts 1:4)

Once they were filled with the Holy Spirit the apostles became amazing, bold proclaimers of the Gospel and made the lame walk again, the blind see, and the deaf hear. In the spiritual world, nothing is impossible - the apostles were even reported to have raised the dead! Peter raised the disciple Tabitha from the dead (Acts 9:40) and Paul raised a young man named Eutychus from the dead. (Acts 20:10).

Jesus Christ came to our world fully divine with God's spirit to bring God to a personal level to mankind, and to die on the cross to redeem us for our sins. Jesus was the perfect human being, precisely what God wanted man to be: the wise, humble, compassionate Savior that was without sin and able to perform incredible miracles. Jesus says in John 14 that He is in the Father and the Father is in Him.

Philip said, "Lord, show us the Father and that will be enough for us." Jesus answered: "Don't you know me, Philip, even after I have been among you such a long time? Anyone who has seen me has seen the Father. How can you say, 'Show us the Father'? Don't you believe that I am in the Father, and that the Father is in me? The words I say to you I do not speak on my own authority. Rather, it is the Father, living in me, who is doing his work. Believe me when I say that I am in the Father and the Father is in me; or at least believe on the evidence of the works themselves." (John 14:8-11)

Jesus' own ministry did not begin until John the Baptist baptized Him in the Jordan River and the Holy Spirit came upon Him. After receiving the Holy Spirit Jesus began performing His many miracles. Jesus told the apostles that the holy spirit would speak through them in troubled times.

"On my account you will be brought before governors and kings as witnesses to them and to the Gentiles. But when they arrest you, do not worry about what to say or how to say it. At that time you will be given what to say, for it will not be you speaking, but the Spirit of your Father speaking through you." (Matthew 10: 18-20)

In addition to Paul writing in Ephesians about the power of the Holy Spirit, in Galatians he writes that the Holy Spirit turns us away from life in the flesh and towards the spiritual.

So I say, walk by the Spirit, and you will not gratify the desires of the flesh. For the flesh desires what is contrary to the Spirit, and the Spirit what is contrary to the flesh. They are in conflict with each other, so that you are not to do whatever you want. But if you are led by the Spirit, you are not under the law. (Galatians 5:16-18)

He ends with listing the nine "fruits of the spirit" that Christians have come to know well:

But the fruit of the Spirit is love, joy, peace, forbearance, kindness, goodness, faithfulness, gentleness and self-control. Against such things there is no law. Those who belong to Christ Jesus have crucified the flesh with its passions and desires. (Galatians 5:22-24)

Having the Holy Spirit is merely accessing your conduit to God; taking your built-in power cord, your subconscious mind (that accesses your spirit), and plugging into God, the power source. It will make your faith soar – just as it did for the apostles when they performed the miracles that are documented in the Bible.

Jesus said he was the light, and talked about his followers being in the light. It is when they were connected to God that they became the light – a beacon for all to see to glorify God.

When Jesus spoke again, he said, "I am the light of the world. Whoever follows me will never walk in darkness, but will have the light of life." (John 8:12)

For you were once darkness, but now you are light in the Lord. Live as children of light (Ephesians 3:8)

Christians that depend upon their own knowledge, wisdom, and religious acts do not have the power of God working for them. Seek the Holy Spirit to awaken the light within you and make that connection to God. It will fill you with faith, love and kindness while giving you greater patience, peace, wisdom, and intuitive knowledge.

FAITH AND THE POWER
OF BELIEVING

"Making things happen in your life requires a faith, or an ability to believe that is unshakable, regardless of your circumstances". (Les Brown, Motivational Speaker)

"I tell you the truth, if you have faith as small as a mustard seed, you can say to this mountain, 'Move from here to there' and it will move. Nothing will be impossible for you." *(Matthew 17:20)*

Having complete faith, the faith of Christ, is the second of our four cornerstones. The Book of Hebrews tells us that Jesus Christ is better than anything religion offers, and that we should put Him directly in our sights: *Fixing our eyes on Jesus, the pioneer and perfecter of faith… (Hebrews 12:2).* At the time, because of the persecution of Christians, many Jews were slowly retreating back to Judaism, and the writer of the letter (in question, but most assume it is Paul) simply says to look at Jesus. He is saying, how can you witness Christ, his teachings and his works, and retreat back to your old religion? It is a good question to ask even in our current world. If you read the words of Christ and believe that He came to us as God in the flesh, how can you retreat back to your old ways? Why do you not conduct your life as Jesus taught us? Why are you not emboldened to be the person who Jesus said you could be?

Believing in Jesus makes us reborn and gives us a new reason for living. Being reborn gives us unlimited access to the Holy Spirit in us and we begin down the path to being more Christ-like. But many Christians, although they are devout Believers, try and try but never seem to grow deeper in faith. So, why can't they get any closer to being the Godly person they want to be and strive to be?

A Pastor of mine once told a story of being a graduate assistant at a college. The college had a Christmas party and each faculty member was called up and given an envelope that was found to contain a bonus check. The Pastor and a friend, who was also a Graduate Assistant, watched as other graduate assistants received checks, and eagerly awaited being called up. Their names were eventually called and they did receive an envelope, but when they opened them there were no checks inside. It seemed these two grad assistants didn't warrant a bonus! As grad students, they both had little money and were absolutely crushed. After being called up and given an envelope they believed contained the same bonus as the others, it seemed almost cruel.

Now the Pastor paused his story and asked, *"Have you ever felt the same way about Christianity?"* The story was meant to show us the difference in what we expect once we become Believers, and what reality sometimes turns out to be. We have been given a wonderful gift from God; He gives us grace and washes away our sins for us to receive eternal life with the expectation that we will follow Christ's teachings and become more Christ-like. The expectations we have about how our lives will change as we incorporate this gift from God are enormous; we eagerly anticipate soaring to new spiritual heights while we follow Jesus and his teachings. So why does it not always happen for us? Why do we still sin consistently and feel the guilt and shame associated with sin? Why are we unable to elevate our conscious thoughts to a higher level and become the people we all want to be?

Negative programming plays a big part, but it is also the routine of daily life; trying to keep your head above water while dealing with financial, work, or family issues can be overwhelming and very stressful. Everyday problems and life itself always seem to get in the way. Frustrations, fear, and human emotions always seem to move us two steps back from the one step forward we achieved. Many times we know while we are doing something that it is wrong, selfish, petty, rude, etc., but fear, frustration, or exhaustion gets the better of us and we do it anyway. We fail in our daily efforts despite trying extremely hard and accept the fact that it will always be this way because we are human.

Positive thinking, seeing the best in your future and in every-day situations to combat life's everyday problems, is one thing that can help to elevate our thinking. The Minister Norman Vincent Peal wrote the book *"The Power of Positive Thinking"* in 1952 and followed it with several other similar books. One of his many great quotes is, *"What the mind can conceive and believe, and the heart desire, you can achieve."* Positive thinkers see learning opportunities in problems instead of defeat and are optimistic for their future endeavors. But positive thinking is merely a component of Believing like Christ, which takes positive thinking to another level with the rock-solid faith that Christ had.

To get to that next level we try to be more like Christ, to live as He told us, but it seems so difficult. The lifestyle and path He set for us are very difficult to conform to. We are constantly reminded that we are sinners, and because of our humanity, there is nothing we can do about it. Many sermons are delivered with the same message, of the many ways that we fall short in the eyes of God. As part of the Christian faith, we are encouraged to acknowledge our failures and sins and to ask God for forgiveness.

Acknowledging that you are a sinner is a basic tenement of Christianity, and we will always be sinners; however, thinking that we can never diminish our sins because of our humanity is a major roadblock for us on God's intended path. We are taught to be more like Christ spiritually and morally; to pray, to praise and obey the Father, to be humble, to be kind to strangers, to help the poor and the sick, and to love thy neighbor. But why are we not taught to believe like Jesus – a no holds barred type of faith that will reduce fear and doubt in our lives? We are taught to believe *in* Jesus, but not to believe *like* Jesus. In Matthew 22:37, Jesus said, *"Love the Lord your God with all your heart and with all your soul and with all your mind."* This direct reference to your conscious thoughts is because God gave us this wonderful brain, this supercomputer mind, for a reason – to be able to commune directly with Him through your mind and your spirit!

Spiritual thinking is an integral part of a truly deep faith. It is not just believing in Christ but also believing like Christ that gives us a complete blueprint to guide us in our journey of faith. It is the daily faith that God will respond to your goals and dreams and make them a reality. I tell people that the day you think to yourself *"This is an amazing world we live in"* is the day you know you are believing like Christ.

Emotions are part of a deep faith and have a strong effect on your beliefs. Believing like Christ involves the heart as well as the mind, for true belief comes from the heart. An emotional conviction must accompany the thought to cement it and truly believe; it is a combination of thought and emotion that creates the belief. It is almost as if the conviction and resulting emotional response acts as the catalyst to make the thought a strong belief for an individual.

You can have thoughts that carry no emotional response and they will not affect any outcome. For instance, you can state that you believe something over and over again, but if "in your heart" you feel the opposite is true, you will never truly believe it. But believing "from the heart" feels as if it comes directly from the soul, and it does indeed become magical. It gives a kick start to sending out your message, your request, or your prayer to the world to make it happen, just as you believed. Hebrews Chapter 11 defines faith (the only time in the Bible) and states that without it you cannot please God and that you must believe that He will reward your faith:

> *Now faith is confidence in what we hope for and assurance about what we do not see. (Hebrews 11:1)*

> *And without faith it is impossible to please God, because anyone who comes to him must believe that he exists and that he rewards those who earnestly seek him. (Hebrews 11:6)*

Jesus talked in parables in many of his teachings, but when he talked about believing and what that can accomplish, he was quite direct and clear. From the Gospel of Matthew, Jesus said:

"I tell you the truth, if you have faith and do not doubt, not only can you do what was done to the fig tree (Jesus made the tree wither on command), *but also you can say to this mountain, 'Go, throw yourself into the sea,' and it will be done. If you believe, you will receive whatever you ask for in prayer."*

Almost two thousand years ago Jesus told us about the power of believing, but even now few realize how powerful and important these words were. The mountain Jesus refers to is simply whatever your problem may be, even if it appears to be the size of a mountain. His statement is a testament to the power of believing and the magnitude of what our capabilities are. Even though it seems completely outrageous, Jesus was telling us of the incredible abilities that God has bestowed upon each of us when we are connected to God and have true faith. These abilities are far, far beyond what we can conceive of ourselves. In the Old Testament, Solomon wrote in 970 BC that your thoughts determine who you are:

For as he thinks within himself, so he is. (Proverbs 23:7)

Thoughts are very powerful and can work either for you or against you; so if things are not working out in your life, keep your focus on God and Jesus, and change your thoughts to believe like Christ. Whatever it is you want and want to be, God is waiting for you to ask. Remember Jesus' words in the Gospel of Matthew.

"Ask and it will be given to you; seek and you will find, knock and the door will be opened for you. For everyone who asks receives; he who seeks finds; and to him who knocks, the door will be opened." (Matthew 7:7–8)

There is a door that stands in the way of our reaching the Kingdom of God and Jesus told us that all we have to do is knock and it will be opened. That knock is symbolic of nothing more than complete faith in God. In Matthew 18:3, Jesus says, *"Truly I tell you, unless you change and become like little children, you will never enter the kingdom of heaven."* He is referring to innocence and faith, like the complete unwavering faith of a child. When you have true faith, God responds to any situation or condition you are in such as fear, grief, despair, sickness, disease, or poverty. Not just a belief in Jesus or in God, but complete faith that God will respond to your request. I believe that God purposely designed our world in this manner, that absolute faith in Him is rewarded in the fullest, for it is then that we are honoring God to the fullest.

Many people misinterpret Jesus each time he says to believe as meaning "believe in me", i.e., believing that He is the Son of God. What he meant was that you should believe in God's ability to make happen whatever it is that you want; to have complete faith that God will respond to your thought or prayer. Scripture doesn't say all things are possible by simply believing Jesus is the son of God. Proverbs 3:5 says *Trust in the lord with all your heart and lean not on your own understanding.* Jesus was seeking that trust, that He can heal you. God responds to anyone who believes as Jesus did.

The Gospels document more than 30 specific individuals that Jesus healed, including the blind, lepers, the deaf and mute, the paralyzed, and those possessed by demons. In each case before healing the person he first asks them if they believe. As an example, from the book of Matthew:

> When he had gone indoors, the blind men came to him, and he asked them, "Do you believe that I am able to do this?" "Yes, Lord," they replied. Then he touched their eyes and said, "According to your faith let it be done to you"; and their sight was restored... Matthew 9:28–29

When the Centurion wanted Jesus to heal his servant and said, "... *just say the word, and my servant will be healed*", Jesus responded, saying, *"Truly I tell you, I have not found anyone in Israel with such great faith... Go! Let it be done just as you believed it would." And his servant was healed at that moment.* (Matthew 8: 8-13)

The Roman Centurion was not a Believer at the time; it was the Centurion's faith in the ability of Jesus to heal his servant that He was seeking. In fact, the Centurion's belief was one of only two times in the

Bible that Jesus was said to have been astonished or amazed. Ironically, the second time was when Jesus came back to his hometown of Nazareth; He was amazed at the peoples' *lack* of faith and subsequently did very few miracles.

> *"Isn't this the carpenter's son? Isn't his mother's name Mary, and aren't his brothers James, Joseph, Simon and Judas? Aren't all his sisters with us? Where then did this man get all these things?" And they took offense at him. But Jesus said to them, "A prophet is not without honor except in his own town and in his own home." And he did not do many miracles there because of their lack of faith. (Matthew 13: 55-58)*

Believing like Christ turns the old adage of *seeing is believing*, into *believing is seeing*. Remember the story of Thomas, where we get the term "Doubting Thomas". Thomas says he won't believe until he not only sees but actually touches the nail marks in Jesus' hands and side. When Jesus appears and Thomas sees Him, Jesus says, *"Blessed are those who have not seen and yet have come to believe." (John 20:29)*. There is something truly spiritual and magical in the power of believing.

The power of believing has also been well known in the secular world for over one-hundred years, starting early in the 20th century, and many books have been written with similar themes. In 1910 in Wallace D. Wattles' book *The Science of Getting Rich*, he detailed the importance of faith and believing in developing success in life. In the 1920's and 30's Charles Haanel wrote many books on believing and success, including *Cause and Effect*, and in the 1940s, Claude Bristol wrote *The Magic of Believing*, which directly linked believing to success in all your goals and dreams. In the late 1950s, Dr Joseph Murphy wrote *The Power of the Subconscious Mind*, in which he writes,

> *All your experiences, events, conditions, and acts are the reactions of your subconscious mind to your thoughts. Remember, it is not the thing believed in, but the belief in your own mind, which brings about the result. Cease*

believing in the false beliefs, opinions, super-stitions, and fears of mankind. Begin to believe in the eternal verities and truths of life, which never change. Then, you will move onward, upward, and Godward.

We need to not only understand our inherent capabilities but to also believe fully in them to move towards greatness, using the faith of Christ. Believing completely as Jesus did, having complete faith in God during our lives on earth, we can use His power to do amazing things because God responds to true faith in an amazing way!

Our lives are truly a manifestation of how we view ourselves. Our subconscious mind takes its instructions from our conscious thoughts and deep-rooted memories and seeks to reach an equilibrium with our conscious mind's expectations. So, renew your mind and believe fully each and every day in the power of God to respond to your requests, hopes, and dreams.

THE SUPERCOMPUTER

"The human brain has 100 billion neurons, each neuron connected to 10 thousand other neurons. Sitting on your shoulders is the most complicated object in the known universe." Michio Kaku (American Physicist)

To propel our efforts to communicate with God, to be more Christ-like, and to be successful in this life, God has bestowed upon each of us the most technologically advanced and powerful computer on the face of the earth, the human brain. It possesses more computational power and speed than the best supercomputers ever built. As of January 2020, the fastest supercomputer in the world was located in the United States, surpassing the previous record-holder in Guangzhou, China; it has a maximum processing speed of 200 quadrillion calculations per second (a quadrillion is 1,000 trillion). Quite impressive, but not when compared to the human brain which operates five times faster. It is estimated that the human brain operates at 1,000 quadrillion (a Quintillion) calculations per second. That is a one followed by 18 zeroes! That would seem almost inconceivable until we remember Genesis 1:27, that God made us in His image.

This is easier to comprehend when you realize that your brain has billions of neurons, which are the neural transmitters that send information to other nerve cells, muscles, and gland cells. In fact, your brain has one-hundred billion neural transmitters, but the truly amazing part is that each of those neurons reaches out and connects with thousands of other neurons. The result is that you have over ONE HUNDRED TRILLION neural connections in your brain. To visualize how big of a number 100 trillion is, a stack of 1,000 one-dollar bills is a little over 4 inches high. A stack of 100 trillion one-dollar bills is 63,000 miles high – over a quarter of the way to the moon. The average spiral galaxy has about 500 billion stars, so your brain has 200 galaxies worth of stars in neural connections. These neurons and their connections make processing much more efficient than man-made supercomputers.

Remember that your mind has a conscious component and a subconscious component, and that it is your subconscious mind that is the incredible supercomputer. It coordinates millions of functions for both your body and your mind every second. Most people have heard the expression that you only use approximately ten percent of your brain capacity; however, that is a myth, because it has been proven that if you lose the functionality of any portion of your brain through an accident, you suffer physical or mental consequences. For over a decade Magnetic Resonance Imaging (MRI) technology has allowed scientists to monitor brain functions through a display. They can see the brain at work and know which functions of the body occur in which area of the brain. The correct statement is that your conscious mind and your daily thoughts use only about 10 percent of the brain's computing power.

Your supercomputer subconscious mind uses the other 90%. It waits on your conscious mind for programming instructions because your conscious mind is your built-in programmer. It tells the subconscious mind who you are, what you believe, what your goals are, what you want, and what you think of yourself. The subconscious mind takes those programming instructions and uses its incredible powers and God's creation to make whatever you believe happen. Henry Ford once stated, *"You are who you think you are"*, and it is spot-on. The path that you follow in life is a direct result of your thoughts at both the conscious and subconscious levels; it is essentially your perception of yourself and your life.

SPIRITUAL COMMUNICATION

Our world is not just a physical world. The Bible tells us that God is spirit (John 4:24) and that a spiritual realm coexists with our physical world (2 Corinthians 4:18). The spiritual world includes a vast communication system that uses your subconscious mind as a receiver-transmitter, and it is activated by faith. This is how faith makes things happen in the physical world, through a direct link to the spiritual realm. Think of it as similar to a Wide Area Network (WAN), which is a network that links computers across wide boundaries such as a county, city, or even nation; and God's WAN communicates to everything in the universe!

I believe that we are all connected somehow in the spiritual realm through our spirit and mind. Perhaps people and our world are like the giant sequoias of California, some of the largest trees on earth. Although they are gigantic in stature (some are over three-hundred feet), their root systems are actually extremely shallow, going just below the surface. These trees grow in large groves, similar to pine trees, and although it seems hard to believe, their roots actually intertwine with the surrounding trees under the ground. Just as we would hold hands to steady one another, they help each other stand strong in bad weather and strong winds, holding each other up. You cannot see it, and would probably never imagine it, but they are connected.

That is amazing to me; to realize that these giant trees, some of the largest living things on the planet, are all holding hands to support each other. I believe that humans are all holding hands with each other through our spirit and God's network, that we are all connected under the surface of our physical world and do not even realize it. It is the power of God's creation at work for us to experience!

Miracles happen every day; prayers are answered and cancer and other diseases simply vanish. Some people would call answered prayers coincidences, but I believe there is no such thing as a coincidence. What appear to be coincidences are merely the product of your thoughts and the power of God working in our world. Your subconscious mind takes your programming instructions and communicates to the world through God's network to bring about events and situations that lead you down the path of your thoughts. Are there random occurrences that have no meaning to your thoughts? Absolutely, but an individual is somehow tuned into those occurrences that will lead you down the path that coincides with your deep-seated beliefs of who you are, what you are capable of, what your limitations are, and what your purpose or role is in life. The "coincidences" that strike a chord with you were sent via God's network.

The reality of the world God has created for us is that if you believe you are jinxed or a "loser", that bad things are in your future; your "luck" will be bad and bad things will continually happen to you. If you believe you are clumsy, you will continually trip, knock things over, and embarrass yourself in front of people. Your thoughts will make it a certainty. It is not a conscious decision on your part, but instructions from your subconscious mind will lead you to the situations and actions that will make your clumsiness a certainty. Your subconscious mind takes your programming instructions and makes it happen without your awareness!

Conversely, if you are confident, believe you will be successful, and see a good future for yourself, good things or "good luck" will happen to you. Your subconscious mind will use God's system of communication and create your reality based on how you see yourself in this world. It will create the environment and circumstances necessary to bring about the desired outcome. So, to increase your "luck", believe as Christ did. Another quote from Henry Ford puts it succinctly, *"The man that says he can and the man who says he can't, are both right"*.

FUNCTIONS.

The subconscious mind has five primary functions which are discussed below.

Involuntary

The first function of the subconscious mind is to regulate your involuntary bodily functions, such as heart rate, respiratory rate, blood pressure, immune system, hormones, blood sugar, muscles and coordination, etc. The list goes on and on, as it communicates and coordinates all your bodily functions down to the cellular level. It controls what is called the homeostatic impulse. This function keeps you breathing and your heart beating regularly; it keeps your body temperature at roughly 98.6 degrees Fahrenheit and maintains a balance of hundreds of chemicals in your nervous system. Your subconscious mind controls trillions of cells in your body and it is as precise and perfect in its calculations as any known supercomputer. For example, it coordinates all your muscle movements without your conscious thoughts. Based on muscle-memory, for most tasks that you are attempting, such as picking up a cup, it knows exactly how far to move your arm, which muscles to contract, and by exactly how much to complete your task.

Memory

The second primary function of the subconscious mind is to serve as a massive data storage file that your conscious mind accesses for long-term memory retrieval (short-term memory is stored in the conscious mind). By the age of twenty-one you have amassed more knowledge than over 100GB of data in your brain, and it is all there in your perfect subconscious mind storage; however, your conscious mind occasionally has trouble accessing it. Under hypnosis, when the conscious mind is bypassed to get straight to the subconscious, people often have total recall with full clarity of events long in the past, even remembering the smallest of details.

Why is it that some people can remember vivid details of a prior experience while others barely remember being there? Why is it that sometimes you remember things better than other times? The mind has phenomenal memory capabilities that are largely untapped, and scientists believe that most of the data and memories are there; it is the ability to retrieve them that is the problem. For example, many times when you try to remember things, you are unable to recall what you want, but hours or even days later, you remember it. This happens to all of us. While it seems that even though you can't retrieve it right away, your subconscious mind continues to work on finding the answer without your conscious thought, and eventually locates the correct "data folder" in your mind. It reminds me of the joke about two elderly couples at dinner. One of the men asked the other, *"Fred, how was the memory clinic you went to last month?" "Outstanding,"* Fred replied. *"They taught us all the latest techniques of visualization and association." "That is great!*

And what was the name of the clinic?" Fred's mind went blank and try as he might, he could not remember. Then he smiled and asked, *"What do you call that flower with the long stem and thorns?" "You mean a rose?" "Yes, that's it!"* He turned to his wife and said, *"Rose, what was the name of that memory clinic?"*

That is funny, but there is definitely a ring of truth to it for two reasons. First, association is a tried and true technique used for memory recall. Associating a bit of information with a picture or something you will readily remember helps us to remember bits of obscure information. And second, for married couples, men generally tend to rely on their spouses for memory retrieval.

A discovery in the last decade of individuals with phenomenal memory powers gives credence to the theory that all of our memories are there; they are just difficult to retrieve for most of us. Highly Superior Autobiographical Memory (HSAM), which used to be called Hyperthymesia, is an ability that allows a person to remember many of the details of every day of their lives starting around the age of six. Amazingly, they can remember exact dates from thirty or forty years ago, whether it was a Wednesday or Friday, where they were, what they did, who they were with, and what they saw and heard that day.

There were approximately sixty individuals identified as of 2020 who have this ability. In 2010 there were only six people in the world that were known to have this incredible ability. On the CBS television show *60 Minutes,* broadcast in December of 2010, five of the six people were brought together to discuss and showcase their unique talents. One of the six individuals was former *Taxi* television star Marilu Henner, who talked about her ability and stated, *"It's like putting in a DVD and it cues up to certain places. I am there again... seeing things visually as I would have that day."*

Research on HSAM was initially done by Dr. James McGaugh, a professor of neurobiology at the University of California. On the *60 Minutes* show he stated, *"They can do with their memories what you and I can do about yesterday ... and they can do it for every day."* Research on HSAM continues today at the University of California, Berkley. It is incredible to think that a person could remember details of every day of their lives, yet these sixty people can do it. How? No one knows, although Cal Berkley researchers have discovered that MRI studies of people with HSAM show preliminary evidence of specific regions and networks that appear different. Of course, if you look at your brain as the supercomputer that it is, the real question is, why can't the rest of us remember like that?

From these sixty people, it can be inferred that all sensory data from every minute of our lives is stored in our subconscious memory banks. It is the retrieval process that is flawed for the rest of us. Somehow these sixty people either retrieve the data differently or have bypassed some type of "firewall" in their brain, or perhaps something in the physical structure of their brain is different.

In another case of phenomenal memory, Doctor Alex Mullen won the USA Memory Championship in 2016. One event for the competitors was memorizing as many computer-generated digits as they could in five minutes. In that event Dr. Mullen recalled a string of 483 digits without a single error, breaking the record of all previous competitions. What makes this incredible memory capability vastly different from HSAM is that this capability was not innate; he trained four hours a day using mnemonics, which is an association technique, to gain this capability.

Interaction With The Conscious Mind

The third primary purpose is the subconscious mind interacting with your conscious mind. For this function, as with any computer, your subconscious mind needs programming instructions. It waits on the conscious mind for those instructions. The conscious mind commands the subconscious for past data, for how to feel, what to think, etc., and the subconscious mind obeys the command. It makes no judgment on the instructions that it receives but carries them out judiciously and efficiently. It even carries out instructions received unconsciously without your conscious mind's knowledge and uses previously defined instructions from your past experiences in lieu of a lack of current instructions. This is sometimes referred to as your "master" programming for your subconscious mind. For instance, if you were bitten by a dog as a child, you may suddenly feel uneasy years later for no reason and later realize a dog came into the room (that perhaps you didn't even "consciously" see at the time). In any situation, if you are thinking negatively, worried about something, or thinking bad things will happen to you, your subconscious mind takes those thoughts as programming instructions and begins to carry out those instructions.

Your subconscious mind knows your comfort zones and it works to keep you in them to minimize fear and discomfort. This is simply your subconscious mind responding to its programming instructions, i.e., making you who you believe yourself to be. It will take you to every aspect of the level of life that you believe yourself to be at, mentally, physically, emotionally, and spiritually. The key is to break that habit and try to reach out beyond your comfort zone. Do not accept an ordinary existence. Seek high goals, have complete faith, and demand excellence from yourself in every facet of your life.

The subconscious mind is always running in the background, sizing up situations and making perfect calculations and conclusions. Your subconscious mind will wake you up in the middle of the night to remind you of something important that had you worried, or perhaps you had forgotten to take action on. This "overtime" work while you are sleeping also manifests itself in another way - dreams. Dreams are merely images, symbols, and themes that are the result of your subconscious mind working continuously, in many cases from what is on your mind and what is worrying you.

Malcolm Gladwell, in his 2005 book *Blink: The Power of Thinking without Thinking*, described a fascinating experiment conducted at the University of Iowa. A group of subjects were gathered to play a gambling game and the object of the game was to make money. They were given 2 decks of cards, one red and one blue, and each subject would pick a card from either deck. Each card either won you money or lost you money, and unbeknownst to the subjects, the red deck was bad. You would win big occasionally, but in the long run you would lose money with the red deck. It took about 60 draws of a card for subjects to start realizing something wasn't right (that the two decks weren't the same) and by the 80th draw they knew that the red deck was bad news. Now, here is the fascinating part. The subjects were also hooked up to physiological sensors (pulse rate, sweat glands, and respiration rate). After drawing only 10 cards, when they went to reach for a red card (but not a blue one), their pulse rate went up, their breathing changed, and their sweat glands started working. In other words, their subconscious mind, as exhibited by their body's nervous responses, knew by the 10th card that red cards were bad! In one-eighth of the time it took the conscious mind to figure it out, the subconscious mind knew. This type of reasoning and analysis goes on daily in the depths of your subconscious mind without your consent.

Even very small, subtle stimuli affect our subconscious thoughts and decision making. Seeing, hearing, smelling, and touching our environment all affect our attitude, emotions, thoughts and beliefs. For example, in an experiment at Yale University, student participants were given either a cup of iced coffee or a cup of hot coffee and were asked to evaluate a hypothetical stranger that they read about. The students who held a cup of iced coffee rated the person as being much colder, less social and more selfish than did the students who held the hot coffee.

A different experiment showed that people clean up more when there is a slight smell of cleaning liquid in the air, and another experiment showed that if a briefcase was in sight people become more competitive. When interviewed after the experiment, many of the people didn't even remember the briefcase being in the room, but the visual picture from the eyes was sent to the subconscious mind and it used that small bit of information to alter their thoughts, beliefs, and attitude without ever consulting the conscious mind for its opinion. The subconscious mind is always at work, providing information and working to interact with your conscious thoughts. It takes stimuli from your conscious thoughts and all your senses and moves your thoughts in that direction.

Emotions

The fourth function of your subconscious mind is to create, house, and regulate your emotions. It creates the feelings you get, such as love, fear, anger, or embarrassment, in any situation based on your personality, what is going on at the time, and previous events and encounters. It also records the feelings you experience in a situation, stores them, and associates the memory with sights and sounds that were present at the time. For instance, you hear a song from your past and feel the feelings which you associated with that timeframe; perhaps you went to a specific place that had an emotional attachment and experienced a wave of emotions. Your subconscious mind not only stored the memories but also the associated emotions you felt at the time, and it stimulates the body to re-enact the emotions.

Emotions can play a big part in believing and setting the spiritual network into action to achieve your goals and dreams. Intense emotions can act as a catalyst to faith, allowing an individual to access their spirit which results in extraordinary things. When God gets involved, changes can happen quickly!

Conduit

Last but certainly not least, I believe the subconscious mind has a fifth function - to be your direct conduit to God. It is the receiver-transmitter with a built-in antenna that communicates to God. Every conscious thought, good or bad, is taken in by our subconscious mind as programming instructions. In prayer, our subconscious mind acts as the transmitter. Prayer is powerful due to its focused nature, and it is faith that causes our subconscious mind to open a direct channel to God and create the actions that will lead to the answer to our prayer. For an analogy, think of the conscious mind as the flesh and the subconscious mind as the spirit. Think of your subconscious mind as the plug and God as the power source. I believe that the subconscious mind is where our spirit resides, and where the Holy Spirit lives because it is our direct connection to God. It is when we quiet our conscious thoughts in meditation and prayer that we hear and feel God's communication to us.

Be still and know that I am God; Psalm 46:10

SPORTS – THE MENTAL-PHYSICAL CONNECTION

Sports achievements involve much more than muscles, muscle memory, and coordination. These physical traits are controlled by both our conscious and subconscious minds, which together coordinate all our muscle movements, breathing, and surges of adrenalin. What makes one athlete better than another who is physically alike and has similar exposure to a certain sport? Various explanations include attitude, determination, focus, motivation, preparation, and a list of other traits, but all these traits are a direct result of our thoughts. Their physical condition is certainly a factor, but the prime factor is the mind. As many athletes have heard, the greatest opponent is the one between your ears.

Most sports professionals agree that the primary difference between top performers and average or poor performers in professional athletics is their mental state. At the professional level, the general difference in physical abilities is relatively small; the real difference is in their thoughts. A good attitude and positive thoughts lead to positive results, but the bottom line for success rests in the depths of your subconscious mind. The sport is inconsequential, basketball, golf, swimming, even bowling or shooting pool. Once you have learned the motion of a sport through muscle memory, it is primarily mental and keeping full confidence. Of course, extensive practice adds confidence and helps to cement that muscle memory, so you don't have to think about what you are doing – you simply react.

Incredible performances start with a rock-solid belief in one's own abilities to affect the outcome of a contest. Elite athletes know that they have trained hard and have the talent. They are focused completely on winning and hate to lose. They also have one trait that separates them from the rest – they are not afraid to lose. In some instances athletes or teams seem to play "not to lose" instead of playing to win. This correlates to their doubt of the outcome of the contest and, as you can imagine, can have negative effects. As Jesus said, *"Do not be afraid, just believe."* *(Matthew 5:36).*

There is an age-old sports question about success, *does confidence breed success or does success breed confidence?* Confidence is defined as, *Freedom from doubt; belief in yourself and your abilities.* Success comes from a core belief (confidence) in yourself and your teammates that you will be successful on that play, in that game, and in that season. That belief is validated by each successful action, so it is a combination of both, each feeding each other.

Any athlete knows what getting "in the zone" means. Becoming "unconscious" or being "in the zone" generally refers to a player doing something extraordinary and means he has stopped thinking about it and let his subconscious perfect supercomputer take over his body functions and movements. You are on the basketball court and you suddenly become incredible; your rhythm is perfect, and every shot goes in. You feel like you could close your eyes and still make a shot. Your instincts take over and without thought, your movements become quicker, you jump higher, and everything is in sync. You feel almost unstoppable. And then, just as suddenly as it came, it is gone. Sometimes you will hear someone say an athlete "was unconscious" when referring to one who was in the zone, and this statement is a lot closer than you think to what is happening.

Because your brain is a supercomputer, in addition to the millions of internal functions going on, your subconscious mind takes vast amounts of data from your sensors (primarily your eyes) and processes it continually. While playing basketball, your subconscious mind takes the visual data from the eyes and knows exactly how far it is to the basket and uses muscle memory in determining how much to move your arm in order to make the basket. It knows exactly how to position the arms to aim correctly. Similarly, in golf, your subconscious mind knows exactly how hard to swing the putter and where to aim to make that putt. In every case, it is only when your conscious mind gets in the way and the slightest bit of doubt surfaces that you fail. It is also why your "unconscious" streak ends – because your conscious or rational mind decides that once you have made seven, eight, or however many baskets in a row, that you are not talented enough to be doing this - you're only human and humans aren't perfect, right? Doubt sets in, causing your subconscious mind to coordinate that small involuntary muscle adjustment that causes you to miss the shot. Yes, I am saying that your subconscious mind actually makes you miss the shot on purpose! It is simply following its programming instructions.

Programming instructions to the subconscious mind take root and are followed whether they are good or bad. Think about your supercomputer brain coordinating every movement of your muscles. The subconscious mind doesn't make mistakes. You only fail when that moment of doubt surfaces; perhaps you know that you haven't trained hard enough, you believe that it is beyond your capabilities, that you aren't good enough or that others are just better than you are, or for some reason, deep in your subconscious, you do not believe you deserve to win.

When you connect with God and begin to believe like Christ you move away from doubt and fear and move closer to being "in the zone" much more often when you participate in sports. When you get in the zone you have clarity, and you move almost effortlessly. Does it happen overnight? No, but you will see small improvements almost immediately, though it takes a while to overcome your prior thoughts, especially those deeply embedded in your subconscious.

A player who consistently fails or gets injured has unintentionally given negative programming instructions to his subconscious mind. They perceive themselves either consciously or subconsciously as lacking in some aspect that leads them to believe that they won't succeed, and fear and doubt sets in. The negative programming from a person's past can cause their subconscious mind to sabotage their efforts. They may say one thing, but, either consciously or deep within their subconscious, they believe another; their deep core belief, somewhat dependent on the situation, is that they are not good enough – that they will fail.

Many times our sports achievements are limited by negative programming based on what we believe we are capable of individually; however, this limiting factor also occurs across mankind as a whole in the form of a psychological barrier. One glaring example of this was the four-minute mile. For many years, runners came very close to running under a four-minute mile, but no one could quite get there, and the world consistently saw times just over four minutes. This led to the belief among many that it was physically impossible for a human to accomplish. Roger Bannister finally accomplished it in 1954 with a time of 3 minutes and 59.4 seconds. Amazingly, within eighteen months sixteen other runners had also broken the four-minute barrier.

Can an athlete get past the negative programming and become successful? Christ tells us so, that all things are possible to one who believes. It will take significant effort to change that ingrained negative programming, but it can be done using the tools provided, all of which are centered on faith.

5

BAD CODE

Our mind forces are often bound by the paralyzing suggestions that come to us from the crude thinking of the race, and which are accepted and acted upon without question. Impressions of fear, of worry, of disability and of inferiority are given us daily. These are sufficient reasons in themselves why men achieve so little – why the lives of multitudes are so barren of results, while all the time there are possibilities within them. "Cause and Effect", Charles Haanel, 1923.

We have all accumulated years and years of stored memories from times when we made mistakes, when we failed, when we were embarrassed, when we were scared, when we acted poorly, when people talked badly about us, or times when we did things that we knew were wrong. These memories eventually fade from your conscious thoughts, but they are still there, embedded deep in your subconscious mind, to haunt you when you attempt new adventures. These negative memories lead us straight to fear and doubt.

God is the one who created this world and the incredible spiritual communication system that allows us to create our own reality, but unfortunately true faith and the belief of a particular outcome is not an easy thing. The problem in truly believing in our success is twofold. First, as stated previously, are the general beliefs of what we are capable of as human beings that are passed on from generation to generation.

These core beliefs change very slowly through time and continue to have a very limited view of our capabilities. This thought is pervasive and permeates every aspect of our lives, limiting us in many different ways. Think of a small child learning daily about human limitations. Each day they learn more and more regarding what we cannot do, the limits of our human existence. Second, from early on in our existence we are bombarded with negative comments, suggestions, and thoughts. This negative programming extends back to our childhood days when we were told that we weren't good enough, smart enough, talented enough, or could not do something. Incidents from our past that embarrassed us, or resulted in failure, or something even worse, can scar us mentally and cause our subconscious mind to accept programming that suggests that we are not worthy of success or happiness. We are programmed from day one to accept severe limitations on our capabilities, and in some cases, to view ourselves as less than our fellow human beings in one way or another.

This negative programming, acquired throughout our entire lives, leaves us with deeply embedded programming instructions within the subconscious mind. Sometimes these are deep-seated beliefs from previous incidents far in the past that, despite continual attempts to reinforce the new belief, are so strong that they remain with us. Psychiatrists can sometimes bring these out through therapy, but sometimes even when people know the reason for their behavior today (whether it is from a hard life, abuse and subsequent lack of self-esteem, a character flaw, or something else), many cannot escape from the subconscious mind's embedded instructions. For example, this is an excerpt of an email from a person that had a very tough childhood, feeling unloved:

> "...positive thinking only works if your subconscious is working with you rather than bent on self-sabotage. Positive thinking works for you because your subconscious never received any extreme negative programming when you were little, so it is aligned with your conscious mind. You were loved and nurtured; I was not. People who have always had food on the table don't have a clue what it is like

to starve. They can be very sympathetic, but it's just not the same as having been there…the only really important gift you can give a child is endowing it with a deeply ingrained sense of self-worth by loving and nurturing it. If you don't believe that positive thinking doesn't work when there is negative programming embedded in the subconscious, look at (a specific person). He talked a good talk and believed. Why was he not a success? Answer: for whatever reason (guilt?) he subconsciously did not believe he deserved it. Like the rest of us with this problem, his subconscious mind caused him to make poor decisions. There are always excuses, but the truth is that we did it to ourselves, purposely. When there's a conflict, the subconscious always wins."

Believing like Christ and reducing fear and doubt is not going to be easy for those who have had a tough life or a difficult childhood. The negative programming of the subconscious is so difficult to overcome that we must learn to disregard it when it is passed to the conscious mind. It also made me understand how imperative it is to change the way we teach our children about their self-awareness. As we grow older, we mature in many ways, but our perception of our limited capabilities remains. As adults we are often laughed at or dismissed if we dream great things and tell others. I wonder how many innovative ideas were never implemented because people were either afraid of being laughed at or afraid of failure? Remember that our subconscious mind does not evaluate the programming it receives as either bad or good; it merely executes the programming instructions.

FEAR

Fear is not normally at the forefront of our conscious thoughts but it is a prevalent theme deep within our subconscious minds. Fear is described as a distressing negative sensation induced by a perceived threat. If you asked most people about fear they would typically describe some type of safety scenario, but fear is insidious and comes in many forms and levels; it surrounds us in almost all areas of our daily lives.

Fear causes us to be less than the Father envisioned. Fear is the overriding factor that makes us sin; it causes us to be angry, to lie, to steal, to have arguments, to be self-centered and egotistical, to be vain, to be envious, to be greedy, to be prejudiced, to be unforgiving, to have addictions, to hoard money instead of giving to those less fortunate, to have problems in our marriage and with our children, and to have difficulties in our personal and business relationships. Most people believe hate is the opposite of love, but I believe it is fear, and fear can lead to hate.

Jesus equates fear with a lack of faith multiple times. From Matthew 8:26-27, when He is in the boat with the apostles and the seas are raging:

He replied, "You of little faith, why are you so afraid?" Then he got up and rebuked the winds and the waves, and it was completely calm. The men were amazed and asked, "What kind of man is this? Even the winds and the waves obey him!"

And from Matthew 5:36:
Ignoring what they said, Jesus told the synagogue ruler, "Don't be afraid, just believe."

Fear comes from a perceived threat to survival or the threat of failure; it is that little voice inside your head that tells you that you are not good enough or smart enough, that you will not succeed, that you don't have a purpose in life, that you don't have enough money or material things, that you are unlucky, or that things will not work out for you. Your subconscious mind uses your fears and all of the associated negative thoughts as a programming request and creates obstacles and problems in your life; it is a self-fulfilling prophecy. Fear of things places those thoughts squarely in the subconscious and it begins to fester like an open sore. Your subconscious mind takes those thoughts and communicates it to the world, which puts God's network into gear, only this time in a very negative manner.

For many, the fear of the future focuses on money. This leads to stockpiling excessive wealth for retirement and sacrificing giving in the present to the needy, the poor, hungry, sick, disabled, and those in despair. These actions, born of our fears, are in direct contrast to what Jesus taught us. In fact, Jesus tells us that following Him and giving up our materialism will be rewarded one hundredfold in this lifetime.

> *Then Peter spoke up, "We have left everything to follow you!" "Truly I tell you," Jesus replied, "no one who has left home or brothers or sisters or mother or father or children or fields for me and the gospel will fail to receive a hundred times as much in this present age: homes, brothers, sisters, mothers, children and fields—along with persecutions—and in the age to come eternal life." (Mark 10: 28-30)*

The Bible tells us many times that God has given us everything we need in order to lead a joyous and fulfilling life. In the Sermon on the Mount from the Gospel of Matthew, Jesus tells us to deny fear and stop worrying about food and shelter; He says that if you are seeking God's Kingdom, He will provide whatever we need.

> *"Therefore I tell you, do not worry about your life, what you will eat or drink; or about your body, what you will wear. Is not life more than food, and the body more than clothes? Look at the birds of the air; they do not sow or reap or store away in barns, and yet your heavenly Father feeds them. Are you not much more valuable than they? Can any one of you by worrying add a single hour to your life?"*

> *"And why do you worry about clothes? See how the flowers of the field grow. They do not labor or spin. Yet I tell you that not even Solomon in all his splendor was dressed like one of these. If that is how God clothes the grass of the field, which is here today and tomorrow is thrown into the fire, will he not much more clothe you—you of little faith? So do not worry, saying, 'What shall we eat?' or 'What shall we drink?' or 'What shall we wear?' For the pagans run after all these things, and your heavenly Father knows that you need them."*

"But seek first his kingdom and his righteousness, and all these things will be given to you as well. Therefore do not worry about tomorrow, for tomorrow will worry about itself. Each day has enough trouble of its own. (Matthew 6: 25-34)

The Old Testament, in a well-known and often repeated verse, says that walking with God reduces fear:

Even though I walk through the darkest valley, I will fear no evil, for you are with me, your rod and your staff, they comfort me. (Psalm 23:4)

Fear subsides when we connect to God and truly believe and our confidence leads us to an amazing life, but it seems that we all have at least one friend, relative, or co-worker who constantly bemoans the things that happen to them. They complain that the world is out to get them, that nothing ever goes right for them, and that life just stinks. If you listen to them long enough it can suck the positive thoughts right out of you. These people take worrying and complaining to a new level. After all, worry is merely a focus on negative thoughts – expecting the worst to happen. In fact, many people who want to stay positive tend to avoid these people for that exact reason.

If only these negative people could realize that they are putting the burden on themselves unknowingly. Their thoughts and beliefs are creating their circumstances about what happens to them on this earth. We give glory and thanks to God for everything He has done for us, but few realize the depth of the capabilities God has bestowed upon us and how we interact with our world. After all, He created this amazing world, and created us in His image.

DOUBT

We have discussed the power of faith that comes from believing in yourself and in God and His spiritual communication system to make whatever it is that you want a reality. Because of our beliefs in mankind's limited capabilities and our deeply embedded negative programming, deep faith can still be accompanied by doubt. Doubt is the opposite of trust and is a direct result of the barrage of negative programming we face every day.

Smith Wigglesworth was a British Evangelist Faith Healer back in the 1930's that was famous for producing many miracle healings at his Revivals. He would start each revival by stating whoever got in front of him first would be healed, no matter what the disease or sickness, and he never failed to heal them. He had tremendous faith and to keep his faith pure he also greatly limited any negative programming in his life. He refused to read any newspapers or listen to the radio because he knew they were full of negative news; he did not want them to give doubt a chance to grow and affect his faith.

Once Smith refused to let a man enter his house until the man left the newspaper he had in his hand outside. I understand in this day and age it is virtually impossible to stay away from all sources of information, but we should make a concerted effort to limit the amount of negative news we receive daily and its resulting effect on us.

Doubt can start out small like a small seed and, because of the constant flow of negative inputs you receive, eventually grow to the size of a large oak tree. It works against your faith and affects your self-confidence. Of course, any doubt of your own abilities is a major impediment to success. Alexandre Dumas, a 19th century author, stated,

> *"A person who doubts himself is like a man who would enlist in the ranks of his enemies and bear arms against himself. He makes his failure certain by himself being the first person to be convinced of it."*

I love this quote – you assure failure by fighting against yourself! Never speak negatively about yourself and always rebuke negative thoughts about yourself when they come into your head. Why would anyone intentionally sabotage their future success by thinking and speaking self-doubt? Replace those negative thoughts and words with positive ones. The Minister Norman Vincent Peale wrote, *"People become really quite remarkable when they start thinking that they can do things. When they believe in themselves, they have the first secret of success."* We must be resolute in our attempts to negate the effects of negative programming!

Many people live their lives expecting problems at every turn. They believe that expecting problems in life is a rational thought process. They think it will keep you on an even keel to stop you from getting too down on life when you have problems, or from getting too high when things are going well. Expecting problems keeps your expectations low and minimizes your disappointment. When things are going really well, many people are just waiting for the bad news to follow. This thought process of mankind has always been prevalent, but is it how the heavenly Father expects us to think? The good and the bad in life do not have to be in equal amounts.

The Bible tells us that with the renewing of our minds comes a new way of approaching life – that we should live in abundance and in faith, and that we should not have doubt or worry in our lives. In fact, when you accept Christ you come under the provision of grace, where all your sins are washed away. This in itself reduces fear and doubt associated with your past and present sins.

Peter was in the boat when Jesus walked on the water, and Peter had enough faith and was bold enough to ask Jesus to call him over; and Peter did walk on water, albeit very briefly! When he began to doubt, he began to sink. Much like Peter, when we begin to doubt, we too will sink.

> *Shortly before dawn Jesus went out to them, walking on the lake. When the disciples saw him walking on the lake, they were terrified. "It's a ghost," they said, and cried out in fear. But Jesus immediately said to them: "Take courage! It is I. Don't be afraid." "Lord, if it's you," Peter replied, "tell me to come to you on the water." "Come," he said. Then Peter got down out of the boat, walked on the water and came toward Jesus. But when he saw the wind, he was afraid and, beginning to sink, cried out, "Lord, save me!" Immediately Jesus reached out his hand and caught him. "You of little faith," he said, "why did you doubt?" And when they climbed into the boat, the wind died down. Then those who were in*

the boat worshiped him, saying, "Truly you are the Son of God." (Matthew 14: 25-33)

Can we be free of all problems in life? Of course not; Jesus said that we would have tribulations in life, but expecting them at every turn leads to more problems. Can we reduce problems in our lives when we connect with God and believe as Christ did to reduce fear and doubt? Absolutely! It would be a much easier life for us if we reduced doubt and had complete faith in God and His world to help free us of many of our dilemmas. The Book of James states that doubt is an impediment to receiving spiritual gifts such as wisdom.

> *If any of you lacks wisdom, you should ask God, who gives generously to all without finding fault, and it will be given to you. But when you ask, you must believe and not doubt, because the one who doubts is like a wave of the sea, blown and tossed by the wind. That person should not expect to receive anything from the Lord. Such a person is double-minded and unstable in all they do. (James 1:5-8)*

Instead of teaching our children about their inherent abilities, we teach them what was taught to us, that there are limits to what we can do. We instill them with the idea that we can do no more than those who came before us. We wish them good luck, implying that their fate is not under their control and that they are subject to the whims of the world, so be careful! This is not what we should be teaching our children. Instead of teaching them that God has bestowed incredible abilities on us when we stay connected to Him, we cloud their minds with limitations. What would a five year old think like if he or she were never told of the things they could not do, but instead were encouraged to seek out their own limits? What if they were taught that nothing is impossible? What if that which seems ridiculous to us, would seem normal to them? What kind of abilities would that child have compared to children who adhere to this world's self-imposed limitations?

We can learn something from a 17 year old girl named Rachel Joy Scott, who died in 1999 as the first victim of the Columbine High

School massacre. She wrote, *How many of us have enough trust, strength, and faith to believe that we could do the impossible?* The Bible says in many different ways that those that do not follow God are indeed subject to the whims of the world, which most would call bad luck. Without a firm belief that God will respond to any request, we are merely "hoping for the best" in this world, which is not how God intended us to live our lives.

When we rid ourselves of fear and doubt we will become more like Christ: strong, confident, kind, compassionate, humble, and giving. We will love our neighbors as ourselves and help the poor and unfortunate. We will cease to worry about the future when we know that we are not subject to the whims of the world, when we know that based on our thoughts and beliefs that God and his world will provide what we need. For when we truly, absolutely believe and realize the incredible potential of our lives and begin to live it, we will no longer fear the future. Doubts and fears about our family, friends, enemies, money, health, job, and the unknown of the future will dissipate.

Lao Tzu, a famous Chinese philosopher, captured the transition of our thoughts to creating our reality on a personal level in five simple lines:

> *Watch your thoughts, for they become words.*
> *Watch your words, for they become actions.*
> *Watch your actions, for they become habits.*
> *Watch your habits, for they become character.*
> *Watch your character, for it becomes your destiny.*

Our thoughts transition to actions which transition to our eventual destiny. It is not completely internal to us - our thoughts send out instructions to the world that God created for us to make our reality just as we see it in our mind; it makes our stature in life just as we believe it to be. So believe and make it exceptional!

FOUNDATIONS

"Therefore everyone who hears these words of mine and puts them into practice is like a wise man who built his house on the rock. The rain came down, the streams rose, and the winds blew and beat against that house; yet it did not fall, because it had its foundation on the rock."
(Matthew 7:24–25)

Foundations, our third cornerstone, are the basis or the groundwork of your life. They are a philosophy on how you conduct your life; everything you do flows from your foundations. Jesus tells us many times in different ways how God wants us to live our lives and it is starkly different from how many conduct themselves. Becoming successful is one thing; becoming successful and having joy in your life is another. It is apparent that many of the rich and perhaps also famous have no joy. Despite the money, the fame, the fancy clothes, eating at the best restaurants, and taking fabulous vacations, they have no joy. Many are miserable, and it is because of their subconscious mind.

In many cases it is because they are disconnected from God; or if God is part of their life perhaps they know their lifestyle is contrary to the way God intended (if God is not part of their life they are still instilled with a moral compass). Or maybe they used people, spread rumors about others, cut corners, cheated, or did other unethical things to achieve their status. In each case, the secrets lie deep in their subconscious minds and, without their knowledge, their subconscious mind directs the negative emotions and well-being so that there is no joy. They may have fun and experience excitement and other good feelings but there is no joy deep down within. This is why it is essential to stay connected to God and live as close as possible to an honorable and righteous life with a heart like Jesus, replacing untruths, spite, greed, anger, and ego with love, joy, and a giving spirit.

We should base our lives on the foundations Christ presented us. If you are lying, cheating, stealing, or doing other things contrary to the way Christ taught us, even if no one else knows, *you* know; and consequently, your subconscious mind knows and stores that information for future use against you in the form of fear and doubt. You have unintentionally programmed your subconscious mind that you must lie, cheat, or steal to make it in this world! If this is the case, you are fighting a losing battle, so you need to cease these actions and change the course of your life.

For a synopsis of all the qualities that God wants in us, to find the foundations upon which Christ told us how to conduct ourselves, we need look no further than Jesus' Sermon on the Mount. These foundations can be summed up as follows: We should obey the Commandments of the Bible; we should be humble, merciful and compassionate; we should not judge, but forgive people and be a peacemaker; we should relinquish our egos, reject materialism, and love everyone; and we should always seek righteousness and live our lives to glorify God.

Several times during the Sermon on the Mount, Jesus tells us to live our lives in seemingly impossible ways. He tells us we should love our enemies, never get angry with anyone, and forgive someone who continually sins against you.

How can one never get angry or continue to forgive someone for doing something bad to you over and over and over again? Not when we are thinking of ourselves first, when our ego takes center stage – when we are living in the flesh vice in the spirit. We can only get to that point when we release our fears and believe that we can become more like Christ - holy and righteous. When we shed ourselves of fear and begin to think of others instead of ourselves, we surround ourselves with love for people instead of material possessions.

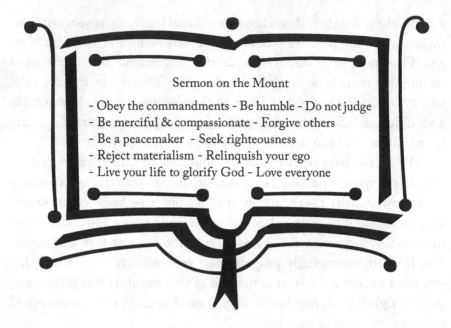

Sermon on the Mount

- Obey the commandments - Be humble - Do not judge
- Be merciful & compassionate - Forgive others
- Be a peacemaker - Seek righteousness
- Reject materialism - Relinquish your ego
- Live your life to glorify God - Love everyone

As human beings we should strive to be as close as possible to what Jesus was, including accessing the spirit of God within us and believing like Jesus, and moving closer to that which God intended us to be. The Bible tells us that God has a plan for us. 2 Corinthians 3:18 says that *we are being transformed into [Christ's] likeness,* and Romans 8:29 states that we *be conformed to the likeness of his Son.* Conformed is defined as being similar in form or type and the root word of "form" means a pattern or mold, so both verses state that as Christians we are to become like Christ.

In Philippians Paul writes from prison that we should all humble ourselves like Jesus and have his "mindset":

> *Therefore if you have any encouragement from being united with Christ, if any comfort from his love, if any common sharing in the Spirit, if any tenderness and compassion, then make my joy complete by being like-minded, having the same love, being one in spirit and of one mind. Do nothing out of selfish ambition or vain conceit. Rather, in humility value others above yourselves, not looking to your own interests but each of you to the interests of the others. In your relationships*

with one another, have the same mindset as Christ Jesus.
(Philippians 2:1-5).

We alter our thoughts and behavior and move closer and closer to becoming that which God intended when we believe. As Christians, we should be focused on the Bible, Christ, and his words. Jesus' last words of His Sermon on the Mount state that our foundations should be like a house built on a rock. He then states if you don't follow his words, you will be *"like a foolish man who built his house on sand. The rain came down, the streams rose, and the winds blew and beat against that house, and it fell with a great crash." (Matthew 7: 24-27)*

Do not hold on to anything that is causing you to live less than a full Christian life. Perhaps it is your hobbies, your circle of friends, pursuit of money, or a fascination with something material. If it is leading you to compromise your Christian life, then you should get rid of it or seek to minimize its importance in your life. Practicing the lifestyle that Jesus taught us is difficult and we will fail occasionally, leading to sin. But continue to seek the foundation that will withstand the storm of today's materialistic and sinful world. As you maintain a rock steady course while navigating your life, always continue to seek the Kingdom of God.

Christians need only look to one of the important messages of Jesus, to fully believe in God's word and the capabilities He has given us, and begin to transform into the people that God intended us to be. I believe that this is the prosperity that we will experience, and it is greater than all of the world's wealth combined. When our foundation is based on God and we heed the words of Christ, we are indeed wise people; as the bumper sticker says, *"Wise men still follow him."* Through our faith in God and what we can do in His world we will reduce our fears, and by following the foundations Christ laid out for us, we will become the people that God intended us to be.

God did not put us on this earth for self-serving purposes; we are not here to accumulate material goods to make our life on this earth easier. He wants us to help others that cannot help themselves, that are less fortunate, in poor health, and those that have had a difficult life. He wants us to help make their lives easier. Jesus told us this time and time again, that people, not "things", should be our focus in life.

Jesus said, "You cannot serve God and materialism. ...For what is highly esteemed by humanity is an abomination in the sight of God." (Luke 16:13, 15)

Jesus said, "For I was hungry and you gave me nothing to eat, I was thirsty and you gave me nothing to drink, I was a stranger and you did not invite me in, I needed clothes and you did not clothe me, I was sick and in prison and you did not look after me.' "They also will answer, 'Lord, when did we see you hungry or thirsty or a stranger or needing clothes or sick or in prison, and did not help you?' "He will reply, 'Truly I tell you, whatever you did not do for one of the least of these, you did not do for me". (Matthew 25:42-45)

Jesus said unto him, "If thou wilt be perfect, go and sell that thou hast, and give to the poor, and thou shalt have treasure in heaven: and come and follow me." (Matthew. 19:21)

Jesus was never one to mince words. He was not the meek man that some seem to think he was because of his teachings on love and compassion. Jesus was bold and confrontational to those he believed lived contrary to God's laws. Think of when he overturned the tables of the moneychangers in the Temple. Jesus didn't mince words when He said that materialism is detestable to God.

He said to them, "You are the ones who justify yourselves in the eyes of others, but God knows your hearts. What people value highly is detestable in God's sight. (Luke 16: 15)

"Do not store up for yourselves treasures on earth, where moth and rust destroy, and where thieves break in and steal. But store up for yourselves treasures in heaven, where moth and rust do not destroy, and where thieves do not break in and steal. For where your treasure is, there your heart will be also." (Matthew 6:19-21)

For many of us, we need to reevaluate the life we are living. This does not mean giving up everything and living like a pauper, or anything even close to that, but simply reducing excesses and using the extra money to help those less fortunate. The joy you receive will be immeasurable. For instance, next time, cut your vacation one day short and use the money you saved to help feed the hungry people of the world. I guarantee you that the day that you gave up will be the best and most remembered day of your vacation.

Wouldn't you like to do something great? I think everyone would! Giving around $80-$90 to organizations that feed the poor can feed a child for a year in some of the very poorest of countries. Giving a small portion of that amount still feeds a child for months. That would be a day that you achieved greatness! The money is insignificant for many people, but literally means everything to a hungry child. I have a plaque at home that reminds, *"To the world you may be one person, but to one person you may be the world." (Dr. Suess)*

Perhaps you could help a homeless person or visit a nursing home and spend time with someone that gets very few visitors. Instead of it being an ordinary day it will be one in which you achieved greatness! Not only do you help someone and bring glory to God, but you get something too - it feels really good. You'll feel like the Grinch when his heart grows three times as big!

We live in a world that is full of greed with people focused not on God and helping their fellow man, but on becoming wealthy and famous. Yet it has been proven time and time again that wealth and fame do not ensure happiness; in fact, it almost seems the opposite is true. Money and fame create an environment that few people can successfully navigate because they have lost their focus on God (we need only look to a few well-known sports and entertainment stars as shining examples). In many cases the rich and famous tend to become the antithesis of what God wants us to be.

We should not get swept up in becoming wealthy, as the real goal in life should not be accumulating wealth and fame, but in moving closer to being the person that God intended us to be - confident, righteous, successful, loving, and compassionate; a person of high integrity whose focus is on God and helping his or her fellow man. Realizing your true potential in the eyes of God is what will bring the happiness you seek. In Dr. Murphy's book he writes, *"Busy your mind with the concepts of harmony, health, peace, and good will, and wonders will happen in your life."* Seek to enrich the world, not yourself.

In striving to be that person God intended us to be, our attitude should be cheerful, loving, and giving, and our resources should be used in a way that contradicts a greedy world, to further the Kingdom of God. The Bible tell us that a giving spirit will be rewarded:

> *"One person gives freely, yet gains even more; another withholds unduly, but comes to poverty. A generous person will prosper; whoever refreshes others will be refreshed. (Proverbs 11:24–25)*

Christ told us that following Him and giving up our materialism will be rewarded one hundred-fold in our lifetime. Does He mean riches? Possibly, as the Bible says you should live in abundance (John 10:10), but I believe He means that when you connect with God and believe like Christ you become truly selfless, as you cease to worry about money and focus your attention on others. It is then that the wealth of peace, serenity, and love will surround you, and all the things that money can buy are available to you, but now seem unimportant.

Aren't you tired of the ups and down in life (especially the downs)? There is a bumper sticker of a quote from Peter Wentz that states, *"If you aren't depressed, you aren't paying attention!"* That sums up what a pitiful shape our broken world is in. Have you had enough of being in a constant state of worry and anxiety? Are you fed up with being hurt, angry, or afraid, and feeling poorly about yourself, your situation, or maybe the world in general?

Depression really is a significant problem in today's world - antidepressant use has increased over 400% in the last two decades, but it doesn't have to be that way. Put your focus on God and elevate yourself to a level of higher spirituality, consciousness, righteousness, and confidence that is rarely achieved and, most importantly, stay there. Think of it – significantly fewer downs in life! I'm not saying that bad things will not continue to happen to you; however, I know that your negative events will be diminished. It is your reaction to life's sometimes bumpy road that will be different. Events that would have caused you to get angry, worry, and be depressed will come and go with hardly a reaction from you. Problems that would have seemed like immense walls before, now look like speed bumps. The popular slogan *"No Fear"* from the mid-90s is exactly what we should feel when we are walking with God, have firm foundations, and believe like Christ: no fear, no ego, no anger, no envy, no greed, no materialism, and no longer thinking about self. When we stand on firm foundations and truly believe that God will provide everything we need, it is not just attainable, it is a certainty.

THE ACTIVE TOOLBOX

"To accomplish great things, we must first dream, then visualize, then plan…believe…act!" Alfred A. Montapert (Author of The Supreme Philosophy of Man)

Our fourth and final cornerstone is what I call the toolbox, a set of active and passive tools you can use to disregard the negative programming and retrain your mind in a positive manner to elevate you towards success. In this chapter we discuss the active techniques.

In my naval aviation career we had lots of Standard Operating Procedures (SOP) that gave you explicit instructions on how to accomplish a task. You had a SOP for practically everything to help keep you from reinventing the wheel, and to make tasks safer and more efficient. Aircrew procedures within the aircraft are very specialized and are known as NATOPS (Naval Air Training and Operating Procedures Standardization), but there are SOP that cover a myriad of subjects, such as flight-line procedures, preparing for squadron detachments, etc. Such is the case for proper procedures when reprogramming your mind and using God's spiritual network for success in life. Just as an engineer or a builder has specific procedures that they use to complete their projects and accomplish their goals, there are specific techniques to help ensure the deep-seated beliefs you wish for and the life that you want to happen will eventually occur.

These tools will help to reprogram your mind to create the atmosphere and techniques to be successful in a negative and chaotic world. They supplement the other cornerstones of walking with God, true faith, and your foundations to wage war against fear and doubt.

CREATING THE FIREWALL

Therefore put on the full armor of God, so that when the evil comes, you may be able to stand your ground, and after you have done everything, to stand. Ephesians 6:13

Deleting bad code from our subconscious minds is a very difficult task, so we must find a way to disregard the negative programming that is embedded deep in our minds. Similar to virus protection software on a computer that creates a firewall to block off the bad code, we will block the negative programming every time our subconscious mind uses it to create fear and doubt. It is the stunningly simple yet profound step of drawing a line in the sand and boldly proclaiming your refusal to accept the thought. When the thoughts of fear, failure, and doubt enter your head you should immediately rebuke them and replace them with a positive statement:

"I no longer believe that. I believe this."
"That was the old me. This is the new me."
"That was then, this is now."
"I will no longer accept this in my life."

You are, in essence, affirming a new way of doing business; it becomes part of your core values that you will no longer accept the fear and doubt that creep into your mind. You take a stand and establish a boundary of thought which you will not compromise. You are saying that you believe Jesus when He said that we should not have fear and doubt when we are walking with God. This is the renewal of our minds! For instance, if you are afraid of heights, have been uncomfortable in large crowds, or perhaps are very shy in social settings, do not intentionally avoid these situations. When that thought comes into your head, rebuke it immediately. You should proclaim boldly out loud that the fear no longer defines you. Stand up straight and throw your shoulders back and assume a stance of full confidence as you denounce the fear! Each time you draw that line and rebuke the fear and doubt that surfaces, it diminishes the hold it has on you.

Your newfound confidence will be like a ball of snow rolling downhill, starting out small and gaining size, strength and momentum as it races downhill. Slowly you will reach the point where fear and doubt are greatly reduced in your conscious thoughts and your self-confidence will skyrocket. It will radiate outwards for all to see like a lighthouse on the shore. It will be intoxicating to your spouse. If you are still seeking a mate in life your confidence will be intoxicating to those you meet. It will be intoxicating to your boss at work, or to employers you are interviewing with. As Jesus said, you will be a beacon of light for all to see.

Fear and doubt are the stranglehold that keep us from succeeding in every facet of our lives, and creating a firewall is a major step in releasing us from their grip.

GOAL SETTING

I press on toward the goal for the prize of the upward call of God in Christ Jesus. Philippians 3:14

The power of setting goals is well documented. Setting clear, specific, and high but obtainable goals is a powerful tool that puts your subconscious mind to work with a task to accomplish. It gives you focus and directs you to action; it gives you a destination to reach. Any management or self-help course or book has setting goals as one of its core teachings. It has been proven time and time again that goal setting is one of the most important actions that you can take to improve your personal and professional lives - it is a classic programming technique. You are creating direction and focus within your mind regarding where you need to be in a month, six months, a year, five years, or ten years; and your subconscious mind takes those directions and puts you on track for success.

To emphasize the point, there have been numerous studies done on the effects of setting goals and there is a science-based Goal Setting Theory. Setting goals was linked to increased motivation and success in the Locke & Lathan book, *New Directions in Goal-Setting Theory*, in 2006. Their research stated that specific and difficult but attainable goals led to significantly increased performance. There have been many different studies and papers written about various aspects of goal setting, and all indicated that proper goal setting corelates directly to success in life. Psychologist Gail Matthews conducted a study in 2015 that showed that people were thirty-three percent more successful in achieving their goals when they wrote them down as opposed to those whose goals were only in their thoughts.

Some of the studies focused on financial success because it is easy to quantify and show measurable results. But your primary goal, both short and long term, should be to establish and maintain your connection to Jesus and the Father. Achieving and maintaining this one goal will make all your other goals much easier to achieve and make life significantly better with incredible joy. Remember that when you stay connected to God, you are a mighty force.

On a personal level, I have set goals and written them down in all aspects of my life (spiritual, family, personal, and work) for the last twenty years. Although some were abstract, I have attained every single one my goals. My relationship with God and Jesus Christ is deeper; my relationships with my wife and children are better than ever; I am slower to anger, more compassionate, and give much more to those less fortunate than myself (just three of many personal goals); and regarding my profession, I was promoted to Senior Vice-President and then to Chief Executive Officer (CEO) of my company. I'm here to tell you that I have personally experienced amazing results in the world that God has given us from setting goals. Results do not always come quickly; sometimes it takes years to modify your thoughts and have it manifest as a reality. Goals should be set high but attainable. Setting goals too low is non-productive, as Michelangelo, the famous painter and sculptor, stated:

"The greater danger for most of us lies not in setting our aim too high and falling short; but in setting our aim too low and achieving our mark."

Think of your life as a journey. Can you imagine starting a trip with no destination? You would not do it because it would be absurd. That is what a life without goals is like. It is akin to drifting on the seas in a raft and waiting to see where the current takes you. Setting goals aligns your subconscious mind with God's communication system. It sets a course for your life, so you don't flounder through life and drift aimlessly.

It does not take a Goal Setting Theory expert to sit down and think about where you want to be spiritually, personally, and professionally in six months, a year, five years, ten years, and beyond; and make sure you write it down to cement that plan in your mind and secure it in your thoughts. Post it where you can look at it occasionally, such as on your desk at work, to remind you of your destination and update it periodically if required. If you want to be an engineer or perhaps an actor, but after two to three years you realize it's no longer what you want, then change your goals. Making a change in your goals is not a negative thing; it is a proactive step to focus on a new area, so you do not end up half-heartedly chasing a dream you no longer desire.

You can use short-term goals to satisfy immediate needs, but they need to be very specific and focused. Some examples of short-term goals would be wanting to save enough money to buy a car, choosing to start college classes, or taking a vacation.

As an example of setting goals to achieve greater success, I had always been an average golfer (around a 22 handicap) and had never really thought about the possibility that it was my thoughts that were keeping me at that level. I finally decided to draw the line a few years back and established three specific goals; to finally score a round under 80, to get a hole-in-one, and to have a handicap under 15. Believing in my mind that it was a certainty, amazingly, I achieved all three of my golf goals within a year of writing them down, without practicing or playing more than usual. My muscle memory hadn't changed, so what was it? I was absolutely determined to get better and believed completely that I was going to be a better golfer. Other players said they noticed a change in my demeanor on the course, taking more time and staying focused. As I look back on it, "coincidences" began to happen to lead me down the path to better golf. A very good golfer overheard me asking my brother-in-law why I couldn't hit the ball as far as he could…so he told me! I came across some internet articles on "mental" golf and other subjects, watched the golf swing of some of the pros in slow motion (repeatedly), practiced my SOP, and I believed.

Jesus Christ had a very specific goal, to fulfill the Old Testament prophecies as the Messiah and to die on the cross for the forgiveness of the sins of man.

> *Jesus said to them, "My food is to do the will of him who sent me and to accomplish his work." (John 4:34).*

> *Jesus says, "Do not think that I have come to abolish the Law or the Prophets; I have not come to abolish them but to fulfill them." (Matthew 5:17)*

Jesus was intent on fulfilling the Old Testament scriptures and the associated prophecies down to the smallest of details, from riding a donkey into Jerusalem to taking all necessary actions to ensure he was put to death on the cross. All in all, Christ fulfilled over 300 different prophecies. Before his death on the cross he said, *"It is finished"(John 19:30),* denoting the end of his mission.

VISUALIZATION

> *"Great accomplishments are always the result of imagination. Almost all world-class athletes, astronauts, and other peak performers are visualizers. They see it, feel it, and experience it before they actually do it." Charles Garfield, noted speaker and author*

Visualization, sometimes referred to as mental imagery or your imagination, comes from the creative right side of your brain (as opposed to the analytical/ logical left side which we use most often). It is visual programming, picturing in your mind what you want to be in life, where you want to go, and what it is that you desire. It is picturing a better future, which is essentially the definition of hope. Visualization is key to embedding your goals in your subconscious mind through pictures to create a new reality. The quote from Fred Barnard, *"A picture is worth a thousand words"*, is highly relevant when it comes to visualization. Your goals are set, and you know what you want in life; now you need to see yourself living that life. Visualize in your mind being that spiritual and righteous person, that caring and wise parent, that compassionate friend, that superior athlete, that confident and successful student or business person, or that healthy and active person, and see it daily.

Your visualization practice does not have to focus on one area of your life; see yourself each day as a combination of all of the above. See yourself as the overall person you want to be and feel the emotions and accompanying contentment and confidence. Remember that feeling the emotions of your visualized success is an important part of the equation. Rejoice in the knowledge that God will answer your request!

You can also use visualization for a specific short-term goal. I remember my father telling me the story of a sales contest they had at work. He was a furniture salesman in Washington, D.C. and had read many books on positive thinking, so he had a positive outlook at work and was always one of the top salesmen. One year the company had a two month contest in which the salesman who sold the most furniture would win a trip to Jamaica. My father proceeded to tell all the other salesmen that they might as well forget winning that vacation because the trip was as a good as his (which you can imagine did not sit well with them!) He set a short-term goal to win the contest and believed that visualization was a key to success, so he bought a book on Jamaica and every night he would look at the pictures in the book for a few minutes and visualize himself there with my mother. In his mind, he literally placed them in the pictures when he would look at the book - there they were on the beach!

You would not think something so simple could make a difference, but the result was amazing; he won the contest easily, selling the most furniture in a two-month period in the history of the company. Every customer that he approached was looking for a full bedroom suite or even an entire household of furniture. It was like he had opened up the floodgates of furniture sales. Two of the other salesmen cornered him in the break room and wouldn't let him go until my father told them how he was doing it. One of them called it *"some kind of a weird miracle."* While it could be construed as a type of miracle, in reality it is simply the way the Creator made our world. Visualization gives your subconscious mind more details on how to interact with the world and get whatever it is that you desire. My father used his belief, visualization, and God's network to help him accomplish a short-term goal.

The value of visualization in sports cannot be overstated. Below are three examples of how important it can be in sports, not just for world class athletes, but also for you and me. It applies to all sports - golf, tennis, basketball, running, swimming, etc.

In our first example, the power of visualization was demonstrated in Dr. Blaslotto's famous experiment at the University of Chicago in 1996. He tested three groups on how many basketball free throws they could make; then for thirty days one group practiced an hour a day, the second group merely visualized shooting free throws an hour a day, and the third group did nothing. Predictably, the first group improved 24%, and the third group did not improve. The startling part was that the second group, those that simply visualized shooting free throws, improved 23%, almost equal to those who physically practiced.

Our second example is about Michael Phelps, who performed at his highest levels during the most important Olympic events because of his mental attitude. In the Beijing Olympic Games the pressure was very high for him to live up to expectations, and he won eight gold medals in the eight events he entered. In both the London (2012) and Rio (2016) games he again performed up to high expectations. Phelps attributes his successes more to his mental preparation than to his strenuous physical training. In an article from the *Washington Post,* his coach, Bob Bowman, stated Michael is the best at visualization he has ever seen.

"He visualizes every possible scenario, good or bad, to prepare for just about anything happening in the pool. If something bad happens (such as his goggles breaking during a race), he has already experienced it in his visualization and knows he will work through it. He also has a complete belief in his abilities."

Our last example is about Aaron Rodgers, the quarterback for the Green Bay Packers. He helped Green Bay win the February 2011 Super Bowl and won the NFL MVP award for the 2011 season; he has been one of the best quarterbacks in the NFL over the past decade. In an article in *USA Today*, he talked about the power of visualization and using your mind to enhance your athletic performance and says that he learned about it from a coach in the sixth grade. He says that *"Foreseeing is believing,"* and attributes his success on the field to his daily mental practice routine. When he is studying game films or lying in bed at night, he says he visualizes the upcoming game and sees himself making great plays. *"A lot of those plays I made in the game I had thought about. As I laid on the couch, I visualized making them."* He had a high level of confidence in making plays in a game because he had already seen himself make the play in his mind.

Whether it is sports, business, your career, or your personal life, visualization is a key to success. It is reprogramming your mind through pictures and seeing your success at your endeavors. It gives programming instructions to your supercomputer, which connects with the world to make it happen. When visualization is accompanied by true faith, eventual success is almost guaranteed!

REINFORCEMENT

> *"It's the repetition of affirmations that leads to belief. And once that belief becomes a deep conviction, things begin to happen".* Claude M. Bristol, American Author

As previously discussed, sometimes believing is not as easy as it would appear to be. Your life has caused you to accumulate a lot of negative programming that can prevent you from truly believing. Reinforcing the belief by continually programming the subconscious mind is the next step. When you repeat over and over again whatever it is that you want to occur, the programming instructions go straight to the supercomputer between your ears and it can change your world.

This reinforcement should be a daily ritual that combats the negative programming and tells the subconscious mind again and again what we want to happen. It is like exercise for the mind and when you have said it enough it becomes ingrained in you; it is written on your heart and your faith begins to blossom. You can visualize achieving your goals daily, or talk to yourself (perhaps on your commute to work), saying exactly what it is you desire and what the result will look like. Examples of specific goals are *"I will become a more compassionate person"*, or *"I will lose thirty pounds in the next six months"*, or *"I will increase my sales by 50% in the next six months"*. You can also be more general in your statement; *"I will be a stronger and more confident person,"* or *"I will be closer to God."* These should be repeated daily, and remember to visualize it as you are saying it.

It estimated that, on average, a person has somewhere between 20,000 and 70,000 thoughts each day, so obviously there are going to be a significant number of negative ones. Negative thoughts coming from both your conscious mind and from deep in your subconscious mind will continue to harass you. Do not despair, for this is quite common and the subconscious mind will recognize that it does not come from the heart, because, in general, only beliefs with an emotional attachment are cemented in our minds. Even so, you should quickly recognize the negative thought and immediately replace it with a positive one that includes an expected positive outcome. Never say, *"I can't,"* or *"I know I will fail,"* or anything similar; replace these negative words with the verse from Philippians 4:13 that we know so well, *"I can do all things through Christ who strengthens me."* It will motivate you, give you courage, and provide you with confidence even in the face of seemingly insurmountable odds!

A key to positive statements is that they cannot contradict what you currently believe. For instance, if you are quick to anger and want to change, you cannot simply state, *"I do not get angry,"* over and over and expect your subconscious mind to comply; it will reject the notion because it knows it is not the truth. You must construct a path that acknowledges your current reality in order to get you to where you want to be, such as, *"I am letting go of the anger inside me; each day my responses will become less and less angry."* Or, if you are a poor golfer and want to play better, you cannot simply repeat *"I am a good golfer."* You have to acknowledge your current poor play and state something similar to, *"Each round I play I will get better and by the end of summer my handicap will decrease by ten strokes."* Using reinforcement applies to all facets of your life: your job, your family, your marriage, your character, athletics and other skills, and your relationship with God.

In addition to Philippians 4:13, the Bible contains many positive reinforcements that you can repeat daily to remind yourself that God loves you, has empowered you to live a life of abundance, and that you should have no fear.

- *If God is for us, who can be against us? (Romans 8:31)*
- *I am with you always, until the very end of the age. (Matthew 28:20)*
- *The Lord will grant you abundant prosperity... (Deuteronomy 28:11)*
- *See what great love the Father has lavished on us, that we should be called children of God! And that is what we are! (1 John 3:1)*
- *Even though I walk through the darkest valley, I will fear no evil, for you are with me. (Psalm 23:4)*

The subconscious mind cannot be fooled, but it can be manipulated with statements and instructions (i.e., programming). One caveat is that for your subconscious mind to truly believe in your request and begin to initiate changes, it has to believe you speak the truth. Consequently, if for whatever reason you constantly diminish the facts, skirt the truth, or outright lie, this will cause your subconscious mind to not believe your spoken words. It knows you tell untruths, so why should it believe what you say? If this is the case with your character, you need to address it and cease telling untruths. Your subconscious mind will begin to trust your thoughts and words and you will then be able to use the new programming to initiate change.

THE SPOKEN WORD

> *"For the mouth speaks what the heart is full of. A good man brings good things out of the good stored up in him, and an evil man brings evil things out of the evil stored up in him."*
> *(Matthew 12:34-35)*

Speaking the words, instead of just thinking them, is an important part of the SOP "success equation". There is something magical about the spoken word. Thinking a thought is one thing, but speaking it and creating the vibrations makes it a part of our physical reality, something concrete. It becomes a creative force that has the power to influence, motivating you and giving you confidence. Jesus told us of the importance and the power of words.

> *"But I tell you that men will have to give account on the day of judgment for every careless word they have spoken. For by your words you will be acquitted, and by your words you will be condemned" (Matthew 12:36-37)*

We need to be humble in self, but bold in Christ when speaking about achieving our goals and achieving success. I told an aspiring young actor in New York that when you go to an audition, you need to be totally confident. You need to talk and act like you belong on Broadway. You need to tell them, "I'm the one for this part". You need to tell people, and believe it, that you will be on Broadway, and that you will win a Tony Award someday. Not in a bragging manner but in secure confidence because there is a fine line between extreme confidence and conceitedness. Always remember that it is through God that this works; God is the key that unlocks the door, so always remember to give Him the glory.

A great story that relates to this is about Ted Williams, a Hall-of-Fame Major League Baseball player that played from 1939 until 1960. Ted was a rookie for the Boston Red Sox in his first spring training in 1939. Jimmie Foxx, another Hall of Famer, was also on the team and was in the last few years of his career. Someone said to Ted, *"Wait till you see Jimmie Foxx hit!"* As a brand-new rookie, having been part of the Red Sox for only a few days, Ted's response was, *"Wait till Jimmie Foxx sees me hit!"* We need to be confident and believe in ourselves like Ted Williams. Putting the spoken word out there for all to hear, leaving you no path to backtrack, is a powerful step in creating a successful journey.

Remember that we said to boldly speak out loud when creating the firewall and rebuking fear and doubt that creeps into your thoughts – *"I no longer believe that!"* You should be bold with the spoken word in many different ways. For instance, Isaiah 53:4-5 says that Jesus not only bore our sins but also our sickness, and that by His wounds we are healed. 1 Peter 2:24 reiterates that thought. I used to get sick a lot, but I took these bible passages to heart and no longer believe in sickness and disease for me, and I boldly proclaim it to everyone.

I believe sickness and disease are similar to the common cold; you come in contact with cold viruses many times, but only get sick when your resistance is down. Similarly, with sickness and disease, simply your belief in them lets down your resistance and gives them a foot in the door. Refuse to accept the thinking that illness is inevitable and there is nothing you can do about it. After I took a stance and began proclaiming that I no longer believed in sickness for me and that I do not get sick, after a few months it tried to get me. I felt sick and I fought it for three days and it finally went away. The second time a few months later it only lasted for a day. There has been no third time. I know a preacher who does not believe in sickness and disease and he has not been sick in over forty years!

It is commonly accepted by most people that every winter you will get a cold or the flu. NO YOU'RE NOT! You watch TV and are bombarded with commercials about which drugs you need to survive in this world to alleviate a myriad of conditions. NO YOU DON'T! Your family has a history of diabetes, so you'll probably get it. NO YOU WON'T! That pain in your stomach might be cancer. NO IT ISN'T! Believe in God's word, meditate on it, believe it to the core of your being, and be bold with the spoken word. My wife has a window sticker on her car that says *Speak to Your Mountain*; this means to use your authority in Christ to speak to whatever problem you are having. Speak out loud and renounce your sickness, disease, poverty, or other problems that you are having. The more you put the spoken word into practice, the more you will reduce fear and doubt and see changes in your current situation.

Putting visualization, the spoken word, and belief from the heart together creates a force as powerful as anything in our world. In fact, combining belief from the heart and the spoken word was written by the Apostle Paul:

If you declare with your mouth, "Jesus is Lord," and believe in your heart that God raised him from the dead, you will be saved. For it is with your heart that you believe and are justified, and it is with your mouth that you profess your faith and are saved. (Romans 10: 9-10)

Jesus says that the mouth speaks what is in the heart. We have already said that thinking a thought is one thing, but that the heart is where true belief lies (and it cannot fool your subconscious mind), so it stands to reason that your spoken words play a large part in believing. Keep "Speak to your mountain!" in the forefront of your thoughts.

TAKING ACTION

"Action is the foundational key to all success". Pablo Picasso

You see that a person is considered righteous by what they do and not by faith alone. (James 2:24)

The next step is to take action on your goals, just as my father did in buying the book and visualizing himself in the pictures. Perhaps you want to be more spiritual, have more patience, be more compassionate, realize a certain sales goal that seemed unattainable in the past, or start a new vocation that you had always dreamed about but never believed could happen. For your mind to conceive that it will happen, it has to be able to construct a path ahead.

For instance, if you are an employee of a company, you cannot simply say, *"I will be a corporate officer of this company in ten years,"* but do nothing towards that goal and expect it to come true. Your subconscious mind will reject the visualization without any action on your part. Similarly, if you tend to procrastinate, but do nothing to counteract the causes or the action itself, telling yourself that you will get better won't work. From *Positive Thinking Every Day* by Norman Vincent Peale:

"If you want things to be different, perhaps the answer is to become different yourself."

When your subconscious mind communicates with the world via God's spiritual network and presents opportunities to you, it is up to you to act on them. You must formulate a plan of action. For example, if you want to be an executive at your company you should seek out ways to improve your situation. You might sign up for a management course, take classes for an undergraduate or more advanced degree, or set up a career path by speaking to your manager about your goal of becoming part of management. You must take action to focus on the little things to be conscientious and work hard at changing your bad habits. Speaking of focus, as always do not forget to focus on God, for it is within Him that all of this works. God is always present and provides for those who truly believe. Remember the words of Christ in Mark 5:36 when he told us to *"just believe"*; a concise summary is to *See it, believe it, act on it, and achieve it!*

Taking action spurs you onward, motivates you, and gives substance to your faith for whatever it is that you want to accomplish. James, the brother of Jesus who became the leader of the Christian movement in Jerusalem following Jesus' death, writes very bluntly that without action, faith is futile.

> *What good is it, my brothers and sisters, if someone claims to have faith but has no deeds? Can such faith save them? Suppose a brother or a sister is without clothes and daily food. If one of you says to them, "Go in peace; keep warm and well fed," but does nothing about their physical needs, what good is it? In the same way, faith by itself, if it is not accompanied by action, is dead. (James 2:14-17)*

James ties faith to action four times in verses 14 through 26, so clearly he wanted to reinforce it. Faith without action is like preparing a meal and then not cooking it. Remember, your subconscious mind must construct a path to get to where you want to go; if there is no action on your part, it disregards the belief.

A famous joke from Fr. Bel San Luis about a man in a flood shows the perils of faith without action. As the floodwater in his town and his house continually rises, he is visited by rescuers three separate times;

first, by two men in a rowboat, then by a motorboat full of people, and finally by a rescue helicopter (by this time the water has risen so high he is on the roof). Each time he declines, saying, *"No, thank you, I have faith in the Lord, and He will save me."* The man eventually drowned, despite three answers to his prayers!

Sometimes God's answer to a prayer isn't quite as obvious as boats and helicopters, but I have read similar stories where people prayed and prayed for the healing of a loved one yet failed to get them the medical treatment that was obviously required, thinking that their faith alone was enough. As discussed previously, you can have deep faith but still have deeply embedded disbelief that works against your faith. Remember that faith without action *"is dead"*. Medical research has done amazing things in the past 30 years. In fact, for medical purposes, God has given us the equivalent of two boats and a helicopter!

PRAYER

"And I will do whatever you ask the Father in my name, so that the Son may bring glory to the Father. You may ask me for anything in my name, and I will do it." John 14: 13-14

Prayer is defined as "a communication with God" that should occur with an open heart and mind. The four main forms of prayer are praising God, requests for yourself (supplication), requests for others (intercession), and giving thanks. Praising God and giving thanks are very important in prayer, and you should practice this daily, but we will concentrate on request prayers in this discussion.

If you believe and have faith in Him, God will respond to your prayer - Jesus told us this. It is not always exactly what you wanted, how you wanted it, or when you wanted it, but God is always good. The answer to your request may even be a resounding NO, but if so, it is for a good reason and eventually it will work out for the best if you keep the faith.

God responds to both thought and prayer, but prayer is the ultimate form of connecting to God through His communication system. In prayer, you are completely focused on God, praising Him and communicating your wants and needs for yourself and others. Requests should be two-way communication - we ask and then listen for an answer. The answer will normally come as a thought or idea that pops into your head and may come instantaneously or sometime later.

Think about it for a minute - you have the most powerful supercomputer in the world between your ears, and you are using it to communicate one-on-one with the almighty creator of the universe. How amazing is that?! You must have complete faith and know deep within your heart that your prayer will be answered. If you pray and truly believe in God's power to respond, amazing results will begin to manifest in your life. Jesus says so with the saying from John 14:13 that is well known to all, *"ask and ye shall receive"*.

Prayer is a powerful thing, and the Bible gives many instructions on how to pray. In Matthew 6 Jesus gives us an example in what is known as the Lord's prayer. In Philippians we are told to pray about everything, to let your request known to God, and to always give thanks for past, present, and future blessings. In Thessalonians we are told to pray continually, without ceasing. And in Hebrews we are told to pray with a good attitude, to be bold in Christ but humble in self. The Bible tell us that fellowship and group prayer are even more powerful. The collective faith and thoughts of a group of people that are focused on a specific request can help to accelerate the response. Jesus says wherever there is a group prayer, he will be there.

> *"Where two or three are gathered together in my name, there I am with them." (Matthew 18:20)*

Prayers are answered with what we consider miracles every day, but God does not respond if it is a hollow prayer or a thought that you want to happen but really expect a different outcome. Your faith must be resolute and correspond directly to what it is that you want to happen. There is the story of a woman whose daughter was getting married in a month. She prayed, *"God, please don't let it rain on my daughter's wedding day,"* and repeated the prayer every day for the next thirty days. She woke up the morning of her daughter's wedding, saw that it was raining, and immediately yelled in anguish, *"I knew it. I knew it was going to rain!"* Obviously, her prayer was a hollow one and she did not truly believe that God would respond to it. Even though she mouthed the words for one result, in truth she believed the opposite would occur. I think it is safe to say that something similar has happened to all of us, praying for one outcome but really believing another would occur. Remember, God does not respond to "hoping" for a certain outcome.

My brother-in-law told me that he prays as if his prayer has already been answered, thanking God for the blessing that He has bestowed upon him. Some would call that presumptuous – I call it true faith; to be bold enough to have complete belief that God will respond to your prayer. It is not always on the time schedule we would like; sometimes it takes months or even years, but eventually events will occur that correspond to your belief. If it is a different path than what you expected, believe it is all part of the plan.

God does not cause bad things to happen to impart a lesson, but He sometimes uses bad things that occur to bring about good and further his Kingdom. For instance, if you are praying for a promotion at work but someone else gets it, continue to have faith and believe that when one door closes, another opens up, and eventually your new job will be better than the one you missed out on. Think about that for a second; despite what appears to be a major setback, you know that God will eventually come through and you are excited about it. That is true faith! That is how we should approach life's turbulent times.

<u>Healing Prayers.</u> The Christian belief of healing says that Christ took on our sickness in addition to our sins (Matthew 8:17) and that by Jesus' wounds we are healed (Isaiah 53:5 and 1 Peter 2:24). There are many stories of prayers being answered through healing miracles. A favorite of mine is an article from the *Christian Broadcast Network (CBN)* website entitled, *"Duane Andrews: A Time for Believing"*. In the article, Duane was extremely ill in a hospital bed and was in a coma. The doctor told his wife Sharon that he would not make it through the night. She had been praying and praying but after hearing that she slid down on the floor and started crying.

It was then that a group from her church showed up with her Pastor. He saw her crying and exclaimed, *"Sharon, this is not the time for grieving. This is a time for believing!"* What an awesome statement for her to hear!

They prayed for hours in full faith and Duane made it through the night and stabilized the next day. He came out of the coma three weeks later, but because of the illness his organs were damaged, and the doctor said he would need a heart transplant and would be on dialysis for the rest of his life. Duane, his wife, and his church continued to pray and pray and eventually he was completely healed. The doctor stated, *"I would say that this process of recovery was certainly not normal or predictable. I have never seen anyone as ill as Mr. Andrews recover."*

Sharon said, *"I would tell people what my pastor told me, 'This is not a time for grieving. It is a time for believing. It's when things look the most bleak is when God wants to step in because that is when He gets the most glory.'"* Duane concluded with, *"I am here and by all medical standards, I shouldn't be. It is just a testimony to God's people. It's the reason I'm here. It's because of the power of prayer."*

What an awesome testament to the power of prayer! There have been thousands of similar stories that involved miraculous healings, and without exception they all involved either individual or group prayer and absolute resolute faith. Stage four cancers have simply vanished with no scientific or medical explanation. Thousands of other diseases have been significantly reversed or completely erased. In fact, there have been so many recorded instances of what were considered miraculous healings that they cannot be discounted as a coincidence or statistically insignificant. After all, something classified as a miracle, by definition, should have a probability of almost zero of occurring. It would normally never happen.

It has been shown many times that people can heal themselves through pure faith. Healing yourself makes sense when you remember the spiritual nature of our world, your connection to God, the amazing power that Jesus told us God has bestowed on us, and how your subconscious mind controls millions of functions within your body. It has been proven that individual cells in the human body communicate with each other. When programming your subconscious mind to accept the thought of healing your body of a particular condition, your belief must come from the heart and be resolute. You must see the healing and experience it, meaning that you must visualize and feel the emotions associated with having been healed. Experience the exhilaration.

Experience the excitement and wondrous feeling of being well again, of being free of disease! Your subconscious mind will send an army of healing cells, or attack cells in the case of diseases.

Many Christians believe that people can be healed by faith through prayer and/or rituals that bring forth a divine presence to heal the disease and/or disability. If you truly believe the ritual will heal you, the healing will occur, yet it is not the ritual but the prayer and belief that results in the healing. Jesus tells us that whoever believes in Him will do the "works", or healings, that He did in his time on earth.

> *"I tell you the truth, anyone who has faith in me will do the works I have been doing, and they will do even greater things than these, because I am going to the Father." (John 14:12)*

A good friend of mine asked a very valid question. She mentioned where devout Christians believed that if they repeatedly prayed, God would heal a certain person. They did so, praying devoutly with the belief that their prayers would be answered; but the person was not healed. Why is that? How could it be that they were full of faith, believing in God's ability to heal this person, prayed daily (perhaps hourly), yet the person was not healed? I cannot imagine and would never tell someone that the person they were praying for did not get well because their faith was not strong enough, or that for whatever reason they could not access God's healing powers, or that their prayer was a hollow one. My friend stated that I have made it too simple.

There are absolutely miracles that occur by a deep faith instantaneously; however, because of various factors such as our upbringing and current beliefs, and the daily barrage of negative programming, sometimes truly believing in a miracle, both the people praying and the person being healed, is very difficult. As mentioned previously, you can have deep faith but still have that slightest bit of unbelief deep in your subconscious mind that works against your faith. Of note is that they are experiencing healing miracles in parts of Africa at a significantly higher rate than in the U.S. because they don't get all of the daily negative programming.

The good news is that there are many ways that God answers a prayer. Remember that there is no such thing as a coincidence. God responds through his spiritual network by creating a path for us, but sometimes it is not a direct path, but more circuitous in nature. There may be multiple actions required on your part to reward your faith. Perhaps they were presented with such a "coincidence" that would have led to the person's healing but either failed to see it as a viable solution or failed to act on it, thinking that the answer to their prayer would be a miracle healing.

The answer could have come in the form of a magazine or internet article or advertisement or a television commercial for a cure or a new medical procedure, or someone mentioned something about a specific doctor to them, or perhaps the path was a little more convoluted; maybe several different things had to occur that did not seem related, and they were expecting something different (i.e., the miraculous healing). The old saying from William Cowper that *"God works in mysterious ways"* could be applicable in this case and in many others.

So, how do you know which rabbit hole you should go down? Which conversation or television or internet ad should you pay attention to? Which one should you act on? If you acted on everything you saw and heard, it would not only be counter-productive, but downright foolish! I believe that with true faith you will be tuned into God's network and He will alert you to the "coincidences" and show you the correct path. After all, isn't that what intuition is all about? For some inexplicable reason, you somehow know something. With true faith, what you think, see, or read about that strikes a chord with you and is directly related to your problem is not a coincidence. Focus on "what" it is you want to occur and not "how" it will occur.

In essence, my response to my friend that said I make it too simple is that Jesus told us it was that simple. You can't just ask for a miracle or merely hope for a miracle; you have to *expect* a miracle. As Jesus told us, *"Don't be afraid; just believe." (Matthew 5:36).* So, pray with abandon, without fear, and with unwavering faith!

THE PASSIVE TOOLBOX

"The secret of living a life of excellence is merely a matter of thinking thoughts of excellence. Really, it's a matter of programming our minds with the kind of information that will set us free." Charles R. Swindoll (Evangelical Christian Pastor)

I n a continuation of the Toolbox discussion, in this chapter we discuss the passive techniques used to reprogram your mind to reduce fear and doubt and activate positive thoughts.

THE PASSIVE FIREWALL

Finally brothers, whatever is true, whatever is noble, whatever is right, whatever is pure, whatever is lovely, whatever is admirable—if anything is excellent or praiseworthy—think about such things. (Philippians 4:8)

In addition to the active response to negative thoughts of fear and doubt, we must also combat the daily barrage of exposure to sinful behavior with another type of firewall, only this time it is a passive response – avoidance. We should do our best to avoid such things as foul language, foul movies and entertainment, heated arguments, lying, cheating, and overall bad human behavior, because all of it seeps down into our subconscious minds and robs us of the joy we should be experiencing. We should think of Godly things, as the apostle Paul wrote in Philippians above. In essence, try to reduce your sphere of influence to good, Godly things as much as possible.

The more you practice the active firewall the less susceptible you will be to thoughts of fear and doubt. The more you practice the passive firewall, your built-up numbness and resulting acceptance of constant sinful behavior all around you will decrease, and your joy will increase steadily as you elevate your thoughts according to Paul's writing. We know that we cannot eliminate all fear and doubt from our minds and that we cannot avoid all sinful behavior in this chaotic world, but as each day passes that you practice these firewalls you diminish them and get stronger walking with the Lord and closer to the Father.

LOVE

> *"Love the Lord your God with all your heart and with all your soul and with all your mind. This is the first and greatest commandment. And the second is like it: 'Love your neighbor as yourself. All the Law and the Prophets hang on these two commandments." (Matthew 22: 37–40)*

In the New Testament faith, hope, and love are the prevailing themes. 1 Corinthians 13:13 states, *"And now these three remain: faith, hope and love. But the greatest of these is love."* We have talked about Faith (Believing Like Christ), and Hope, or seeing a better future (Setting Goals and Visualization); next up is Love. Jesus tells us in Matthew 22 that love is the most important thing for humans on earth; love of God first and love of your fellow man second. I think deep in our hearts we all know this. Love is the eternal truth; it is infinite and pure. In fact, 1 John 4:8 states, *"Whoever does not love does not know God, because God is love."*

Having a heart full of hate, anger, bitterness, regret, unforgiveness, or remorse is a major impediment to success and having joy in life. These negative feelings, which could be directed towards the world in general, to a group of people, or even just one person (including you!), cause harm to your relationships and your physical and mental health, and lead to anxiety, stress, depression, and low self-esteem. You need to replace the negative feelings and emotions with positive ones and bring forth the love that is within you. This will lead to forgiveness, joy, confidence, and success in your endeavors. When you are walking with God daily, love begins to pour out of you like a spiritual faucet.

Jesus is very specific in telling us if we trust in God that He will provide all that we need. We will cease to worry about the past, present, and future with the secure, rock-hard belief that the Father will take care of us. Just imagine the scenario – people everywhere unafraid of the present and the future, fully believing and *knowing* that with an effort on their part, God will take care of them because He created a world that responds to faith. And when our fears diminish, what takes its place? The answer is love. In all of Jesus' teachings, love is a dominant theme concerning how we should live our lives. Love is a natural response to releasing our fears; 1 John 4:18 states, *"There is no fear in love; but perfect love drives out fear."* This is a rebirth of your love of God and Christ, a rebirth of your love for your spouse and family, a love of your neighbors, a love of all mankind, and yes, even a love for your former enemies. As Jesus said in Matthew 22 above, loving God and loving your neighbor are the two greatest commandments.

There is a well-known passage from First Corinthians that I have heard as a reading at many weddings, because it describes the beauty of love:

> *Love is patient, love is kind. It does not envy, it does not boast, it is not proud. It is not rude, it is not self-seeking, it is not easily angered, it keeps no record of wrongs. Love does not delight in evil but rejoices with the truth. It always protects, always trusts, always hopes, always perseveres. Love never fails... (First Corinthians 13: 4-8)*

Think of the spiritual love you feel for God the Creator and his son Jesus Christ, or in earthly terms, the love of a mother for her baby and the love between spouses, family and friends. Most people don't spend a lot of time thinking about love. There is just too much going on in our lives to stop and think about... love? But guess what? In the end, when we are about to die, what is the primary thing that we think about? You guessed it - love. It is well known that on their deathbed, no one ever wished that they had spent more time at the office. They wished they had paid more attention to their family; they wish they had loved better and more.

In an article on CNN.com entitled, *"My Faith: What People Talk About Before They Die"*, a hospice chaplain, when asked, *"What do people who are sick and dying talk about?"* He stated,

> *"I, without hesitation or uncertainty, would give you the same answer (love). Mostly, they talk about their families: about their mothers and fathers, their sons and daughters. They talk about the love they felt, and the love they gave. Often, they talk about love they did not receive, or the love they did not know how to offer, the love they withheld, or maybe never felt for the ones they should have loved unconditionally. They talk about how they learned what love is, and what it is not. Love is almost always the most important thing to people in their lives when reflecting back on them."*

In addition to our family, loved ones, and friends, Jesus tells us to love our neighbor. Most people can accept that, but He also tells us that while it is easy to love someone you like, that we must love everyone, even those we dislike. In the Sermon on the Mount, He says,

> *"You have heard that it was said, 'Love your neighbor and hate your enemy.' But I tell you, love your enemies and pray for those who persecute you, that you may be children of your Father in heaven. He causes his sun to rise on the evil and the good and sends rain on the righteous and the unrighteous. If you love those who love you, what reward will you get? Are not even the tax collectors doing that? And if you greet only your own people, what are you doing more than others? Do not even pagans do that? Be perfect, therefore, as your heavenly Father is perfect." (Matthew 5, 43:48)*

Loving your enemy is a difficult thing to do, but it is made considerably easier when your fears and ego diminish because you are walking in the spirit, believing like Christ, and using the tools presented. A famous quote from Abraham Lincoln is, *"Do I not defeat my enemy when I make him my friend?"* When your heart is full of love for your fellow man this will be a natural evolution towards former enemies. First Corinthians states:

> *If I have a faith that can move mountains, but do not have love, I am nothing.*

Always remember that you have the power to choose your state of mind and are in full control of your actions. You can choose love, health and happiness. You can choose to be a loving, kind friend to all who builds people up instead of tearing them down. Remember that giving a compliment or kind word can make someone's entire day better. Be joyous and cooperative with others, not combative, and people will respond to you with similar thoughts and actions.

PERSEVERANCE

> *"Nothing in this world can take the place of persistence. Talent will not; nothing is more common than unsuccessful men with talent. Genius will not; unrewarded genius is almost a proverb. Education will not; the world is full of educated derelicts. Persistence and determination alone are omnipotent. The slogan Press On! has solved and always will solve the problems of the human race."*
> *President Calvin Coolidge*

Perseverance is defined as *"persistence in doing something despite difficulty or delay in achieving success."* It is a mindset of mental toughness, making a determined decision not to give up when the going gets tough through unexpected obstacles, delays, and even repeated failures. The problem may be a difficult task or have overwhelming odds; perhaps it takes going that extra mile with an extensive effort or getting out of your comfort zone to find a solution. The importance of perseverance and persistence was famously summed up by President Calvin Coolidge's famous quote above from 1929 – always press on!

Thomas Edison's pursuit of inventing the electric lightbulb is probably the most well-known case of perseverance. He failed over a thousand times in trying to find the right filament for the first electric lightbulb. When a reporter asked, *"How did it feel to fail 1,000 times?"* Edison replied, *"I didn't fail 1,000 times. The light bulb was an invention with 1,000 steps."* He was adamant in telling people to continue to persevere, to never give up. He later stated, *"Many of life's failures are people who did not realize how close they were to success when they gave up."*

Patience, persistence, and perseverance are essential qualities for success in life. The Bible says many times that these virtues are important to practice daily, and that perseverance builds character. Below are some Bible verses that relate to never giving up:

- *Let us not become weary in doing good, for at the proper time we will reap a harvest if we do not give up. Galatians 6:9*
- *Consider it pure joy, my brothers and sisters, whenever you face trials of many kinds, because you know that the testing of your faith produces perseverance. Let perseverance finish its work so that you may be mature and complete, not lacking anything. James 1:2-4*
- *Blessed is the one who perseveres under trial because, having stood the test, that person will receive the crown of life that the Lord has promised to those who love him. James 1:12*
- *As you know, we count as blessed those who have persevered. You have heard of Job's perseverance and have seen what the Lord finally brought about. The Lord is full of compassion and mercy. James 5:11*
- *You need to persevere so that when you have done the will of God, you will receive what he has promised. Hebrews 10:36*
- *Be joyful in hope, patient in affliction, faithful in prayer. Romans 12:12*
- *being strengthened with all power according to his glorious might so that you may have great endurance and patience, Colossians 1:11*

Perseverance means not giving up because of failure. There is a well-known saying from Gene Kranz, *"Failure is not an option."* This may be the case in military operations where lives hang in the balance, but this is not the case in your everyday life. The truth is that you should be failing in your life's adventures… occasionally. If you are never failing in life, you are not reaching high enough, not striving for the tough-to-reach ideals, or not setting your goals high enough. You should set your goals so that they are difficult to obtain, but reachable. Your eventual success will then be a remarkable achievement.

You learn a lot from failure; it is a great teacher. Almost every multi-millionaire failed in at least one business venture and many scientists failed repeatedly before achieving success. Failure should not be viewed as an end but as part of a process. Whatever it is that you are attempting to do, you must have the will and the determination to continue on despite initial failures.

While in community college I applied to the Naval Academy through my Congressman and out of over 100 candidates it came down to two of us for one billet. A Congressional staff member notified me that I did not get the appointment but said he could get me into the Air Force Academy or West Point instead. I told him no, I wanted to go to the Naval Academy, and I would go back to community college and try again next year. He looked at me like I had three heads and said, *"I don't think you understand; there are no guarantees for next year. I can get you in another service academy now!"* But I stuck to my guns and went back to school for another year and eventually got my appointment to the Naval Academy. I did not despair over my rejection, and I did not take a second choice. I knew what I wanted and was willing to take a risk and persevere for another year to get there. In retrospect, I took heed of the famous naval quote by John Paul Jones, *"He who will not risk, cannot win".*

Perseverance, persistence, patience, and determination are all character traits of a person who refuses to accept problems, obstacles, delays, criticism, and failure as ultimate defeat and continues to work as hard as they can to achieve their goal. They are essential qualities for success in all your life's endeavors.

SUMMARY

"We know we were made for so much more than ordinary lives. It's time for us to more than just survive. We were made to thrive" – Casting Crowns, "Thrive"

Human beings have substantial untapped potential and are capable of much more than we currently believe. To enhance our performance, we can connect to God through our brains, the most advanced supercomputers on the face of the earth; however, we are held down considerably by the constant negative programming of our minds. It ends up residing deep in our subconscious minds and leads to fear, doubt, and a sometimes difficult, ordinary life. To combat this and elevate our lives to extraordinary, we have four cornerstones to live by:

- Stay connected daily to God
- Have complete faith, "Believing Like Christ"
- Have firm foundations for your life
- The Toolbox, a set of techniques to disregard the negative programming and reprogram your mind with positive thoughts

These four cornerstones are the principles for success in your life's endeavors. Rather than being subject to the whims of the world, the world reacts to our core thoughts and beliefs. Our thoughts create our reality, and to change our circumstances we need to reprogram our minds and alter our thoughts.

If your career or your personal life is, using a naval term, "Dead-in-the-Water" (a ship that has lost propulsion capability), the value of maintaining the four cornerstones, including the tools in the active and passive toolboxes, cannot be overstated. Using the firewalls, setting goals, visualizing, reinforcement, the spoken word, love, taking action, perseverance, and prayer daily in your life will help you to diminish or disregard the negative programming and add positive programming to your subconscious mind. These tools will reduce fear and doubt, elevate your confidence significantly, and help to ensure success, not just in your career but in every facet of your existence; they will help to make you a better human being. Business success and earnings are important but should not be the primary areas you target. Use these tools for your personal growth, for it is there that you can elevate your spiritual life and follow the path that Jesus taught us.

Our world is a broken one, and the foundations that Christ gave us in the Sermon on the Mount are slowly eroding away. Following God, believing to the core that He will respond to our wants and needs, having firm foundations, and practicing the tools provided to reduce fear and doubt will turn us back in the right direction. Sin will become less and less for humanity as a whole and we will begin to heal our broken world.

God created this world to reward true faith, when we honor Him by knowing that He will respond to our request. It is then that our subconscious minds open the direct channel to God and the Holy Spirit is awakened within us. When we do this, our fears about life will dissipate and, because sin is born of fear, we will collectively begin to move toward the path of righteousness. Fear will be replaced by love and we will move closer towards fulfilling Christ's belief that we can elevate ourselves through God to a higher level of conscious thought, compassion, morality, and spirituality. Then, and only then, will we become the people that God intended us to be.

Remember that Christ told us we are the light of the world and that we can do amazing things if we believe. When we tap into God's spiritual network, we enter a whole new realm of what is possible for us by creating a reality based on our core beliefs. As we evolve we will become more aware of ourselves, our world, and God's interaction. Our faith will increase and our doubts will subside. Do not set your sights too low in life, do not punish yourself for past mistakes and transgressions, and do not listen to that voice that says you are not what you should be. If you believe these things then you need to change the way you are thinking; eliminate, reduce, or bypass your mind's negative thoughts and negative memories, believe in yourself, and just as importantly, forgive yourself. After all, God forgives you and He believes that you are capable of being an incredible person in every way – in fact, He designed you that way! So, ask God to make you a compassionate, loving, successful person and believe it will happen with all your heart and soul. Live each day believing it, and it will be so; Christ guaranteed it.

When we trust in God and believe in Him, we are rewarded to the fullest - it is how He made our world. We need to be like Peter, to believe enough to be bold. We too will doubt and sink as Peter did on our first attempts, but one day believing like Christ and the miracles of today will become tomorrow's everyday occurrences.

I envision a world where righteousness abounds; where people are connected to God with elevated thoughts and are completely selfless. It will occur when mankind begins to think compassionately of his fellow man before himself because we have no fear of the future, knowing that God will provide just as Jesus taught us. As we move away from ordinary towards extraordinary, we will think differently, act differently, and move into a realm of enhanced capabilities, reaching for the unreachable. Do not doubt your courage in your attempts, for remember Paul's words from Philippians 4:13, *"I can do all things through Christ who gives me strength."*

ABOUT THE AUTHOR

Gary Bell is a 1981 graduate of the U.S. Naval Academy and received an MBA Degree in 1992. He is a retired Naval Flight Officer and has been the CEO of AdSTM, Inc., a Federal contracting company in McLean, VA, since 2014. He is a Christian and lives in Annandale, VA with his wife Frannie, to whom he has been happily married for 33 years. Frannie graduated from Charis Bible College and received her Minister's License, and together they attend Anchor Church in Fairfax, VA. They have three adult children, Cassie, Ryan, and Marty.

Printed in the United States
by Baker & Taylor Publisher Services

Printed in the United States
by Baker & Taylor Publisher Services